D1557353

THE
AIRMAN'S
WAR

Atheneum | 1982 | New York

THE AIRMAN'S WAR

World War II
in the Sky

ALBERT MARRIN

Photo credits

General Dynamics 16–17
National Archives 12, 22, 114, 130, 131, 136–137, 157, 159, 171, 198
U.S. Air Force 24, 31, 34, 55, 60–61, 67, 72, 74–75, 77, 81, 85, 86, 87, 93, 94, 96, 100, 103, 107, 111, 116, 125, 146, 150, 174–75, 176–77, 178, 185, 188, 201, 202
Defense Audiovisual Agency 122

LIBRARY OF CONGRESS CATALOGING IN PUBLICATION DATA

Marrin, Albert.   The airman's war.

Bibliography: p. 205
Includes index.
SUMMARY: Examines the role of the air force in World War II, including the nonstop bombing over Germany and the slow island by island battles in the Pacific.
1. World War, 1939–1945 — Aerial operations, American — Juvenile literature. 2. World War, 1939–1945 — Campaigns — Europe — Juvenile literature. 3. World War, 1939–1945 — Pacific Ocean — Juvenile literature. 4. United States. Army Air Forces — History — 20th century — Juvenile literature. 5. Aircraft carriers — United States — History — 20th century — Juvenile literature. [1. World War, 1939–1945 — Aerial operations. 2. World War, 1939–1945 — Campaigns — Europe. 3. World War, 1939–1945 — Pacific Ocean. 4. United States. Army Air Forces — History] I. Title.
D785.M35   940.54′4973   81–8018
ISBN 0–689–30907–4   AACR2

Published simultaneously in Canada by McClelland & Stewart, Ltd.
Composition by American–Stratford Graphic Services, Inc., Brattleboro, Vermont
Printed and bound by Fairfield Graphics, Fairfield, Pennsylvania
Designed by Mary M. Ahern & Mina Greenstein
First Edition

To those who were there

Contents

". . . the most important social service
that a government can do for its people
is to keep them alive and free."

—*Sir John Slessor, Chief of
Staff, Royal Air Force*

1

The Lean Years

Noon, July 21, 1921, somewhere off the Virginia Capes. Visibility poor, a light haze creeping in from the southeast.

The battleship *Ostfriesland* rides at anchor, empty and alone, like some ancient sea monster in captivity. Red, white, and blue target circles are painted on her gray hull.

Once she was the pride of the Imperial German Navy. Even today, though she was a prize of war at the end of World War I, U.S. Navy men say she is unsinkable. At the Battle of Jutland five years earlier she had taken eighteen hits from British naval guns and struck a mine. But her four steel skins held, allowing her to steam away for repairs under her own power.

Excitement builds as military men, politicians, and

reporters crowd the rails of the observation ships. Everyone looks up when, a few minutes after noon, the droning of airplane motors is heard in the distance. There they are, the bombers!

They are still specks in the sky, but soon they turn into a Handley Page and six Martins. Lining up in attack formation, they close with *Ostfriesland* at three thousand feet. Each carries a single one-ton bomb slung under its fuselage.

The first bomb glistens in the hazy sunlight, falling straight as an arrow. BOOM! The sound echoes across the water. It is a near-miss that throws thousands of tons of white water into the air.

Another plane goes by. BOOM! Another miss; more white water.

The Navy men are beginning to smile, congratulating themselves that planes can't sink great warships after all. But at 1221 hours* a bomb slams into the ship's bow, bursting it open and sending up tongues of flame and smoke. Two more hits and *Ostfriesland* slips under the waves. Only floating wreckage and ripples remain for a few minutes to mark her grave.

The Navy men are not smiling as the bombers turn for home, Langley Field, Virginia. Their chins drop. Admirals and captains, tough old seadogs with leathery skin and weatherbeaten faces, wipe their tears with handkerchiefs. Some aren't trying to hold back the tears.

* Military time is based on the twenty-four-hour day. Thus 1221 hours, or simply 1221, is 12:21 P.M., and so on.

For much more than an old battleship has gone down: it also signals the passing of a way of life hundreds of years old.

It had been an exciting show staged by a master showman, Brigadier General William "Billy" Mitchell. The showman's aim, though, was not to amuse but to shock. Sinking an "unsinkable" battleship was his way of showing how aviation had changed warfare.

The airplane was to modern warfare what gunpowder had been to the knights of the Middle Ages. It changed everything. And no amount of hope, or tears, or anger could ever bring back "the good old days." As Mitchell told the cheering airmen at Langley Field that night: "Well, lads, I guess we showed old Admiral Tubaguts today! In the war to come, and you'll see it, God will be on the side of the heaviest air force."

Yet Mitchell's joy was not complete. He knew that the United States, which through the Wright brothers had taught man to fly in machines heavier than air, lagged behind every big nation in military aviation. As an officer in France during the First World War, 1914–1918, he had seen what air power meant. More than that, he had looked into the future and seen what command of the skies *could* mean.

Others didn't share his vision. He was ashamed at the poor showing his country had made over the battlefields of the Western Front. Except for the adventures of some "aces" like Eddie Rickenbacker, America's role in the air in World War I had been a story of too little too late.

Strange as it seems now, when air travel is as normal

as going to the supermarket, American's didn't get used to airplanes easily. For many years after the Wright brothers' flight at Kitty Hawk, North Carolina, in 1903, they thought of airplanes as nothing but dangerous toys. Sure, they'd go to a fairground to watch a daredevil do barrel rolls and loop-the-loops. But fly themselves? Or let their children fly? Not on your life.

Mitchell's friend Henry H. "Hap" Arnold found this out the hard way. Arnold would command the Army Air Force in the Second World War, but in 1912 he was only a young lieutenant who had just been taught to fly by the Wright brothers. One day he crash-landed in Massachusetts Bay. He was tangled in the plane's wires and bleeding from a head wound when two Civil War veterans wearing their old blue uniforms came by in a sailboat. Arnold yelled for help. They came closer, looked at him for a second, and sailed away. "Anybody's fool enough to get himself into one of those things can get himself out again," Arnold heard one of them say.

When war came to our country in 1917, we were short of everything that had to do with flying. There was no Air Force, only an Air Section of the Army Signal Corps. And this had fewer than twelve hundred men and 300 training planes; there were no warplanes. The Government saw the problem and by Armistice Day (November 11, 1918) several million dollars had been spent on the air corps, to increase it to one hundred ninety-five thousand men.

America's air warriors did most of their fighting in foreign-built planes. Although our factories built fourteen thousand planes during the war, fewer than 200 ever saw battle, because production didn't begin in a big way until the last few months of the conflict. Our airmen had to borrow whatever they could from the Allies. They met the Germans in French Nieuports and British Spads and Sopwith Camels.

The U.S. Army brass didn't have much use for airplanes. "Black Jack" Pershing, commander of American forces in Europe during World War I, saw no reason why a fighter pilot should be paid twice as much as an infantry platoon leader. But his plan to cut pilots' pay failed in Congress. After all, the voters wouldn't like it if heroes like Rickenbacker were put on the same level as plain infantrymen.

People's memories are short, and yesterday's heroes soon become today's nobodies. Once the "war to end war" ended, people wanted to forget it, like a bad dream. America's armies were no longer needed and were all but done away with after the Armistice. The Army's Air Service, its youngest branch, suffered the most. Cutbacks almost killed it. By June, 1921, only a handful of devoted pilots and ground crew remained to fly its aging fleet of "flying coffins."

Billy Mitchell held the test off the Virginia Capes to show the stupidity of neglecting air power. He believed that airplanes were improving all the time, while warships could not be made any better than they already were. Airplanes flying from shore bases or "floating airdromes" (aircraft carriers) had made navies a thing of the past. "Aircraft now in existence," he wrote, "can find and destroy all classes of seacraft under war conditions with negligible loss." As for the Army's idea that airplanes were useful only as artillery spotters, that was plain nonsense.

Mitchell did not make friends easily in the other armed services. He was convinced he was right, and anyone who didn't agree with him was a fool or a liar.

He could not keep his mouth shut, and he spat out insults like machine gun bullets. His outcry against the "battleship admirals" became so embarrassing that his superiors lowered his rank to colonel and sent him to a lonely army post in Texas. But he wouldn't be quiet. He called the way the services treated aviation "disgusting" and a shame for the nation.

He had gone too far this time. In 1925, Billy Mitchell was court-martialed and found guilty of disgracing the Army. Rather than allow himself to be broken from rank and lose five years pay as the court ordered, he resigned. His enemies were glad to see the "General of the Hot Air Force" go.

Mitchell had nothing to lose now, and began bombarding Americans with speeches, articles, and books about the neglect of air power. And he warned . . . always warned about the bad days he saw coming.

For Mitchell was certain there would be another war. When it would come he didn't know, but he did know that Japan would be the enemy. The Japanese had gone in for aviation in a big way. In 1921, Japanese officers took snapshots of the bombing of *Ostfriesland*. They took hundreds of pictures, many more than they needed for souvenirs. They were also building aircraft carriers, big ones.

During the winter of 1923–1924 Mitchell visited

Japan to see things for himself. What he saw made him say that the United States had better watch its step. The Japanese military were beginning to control the government, and they believed that the U.S. stood in the way of their plans to take over Asia. When they were ready they would knock the U.S. out of the way like a truck hitting a puppy. Mitchell once told friends in his Virginia home: "The Japanese will not politely declare war . . . Hawaii . . . is vulnerable to the sky. It is wide open to Japan. Yet we bring our Navy in at Pearl Harbor and lock it up every Saturday night so that the sailors can spend their week's pay to please the merchants and politicians. . . . And Hawaii is swarming with Japanese spies. . . . That's where the blow will be struck — on a fine, quiet Sunday morning."

When Billy Mitchell died of a heart attack in February, 1936, at the age of 57, the world was a more dangerous place for his country than when he left the Army ten years before. Militarism and dictatorship were on the rise everywhere. The warlords of Japan, Germany, and Italy were working toward taking over the world.

These men saw air power not only as a weapon but as a sign of their own greatness. Their peoples, they said, were nations of fliers: heroic, modern, and bound to rule the world. Adolf Hitler once called the airplane "a manly weapon, a Germanic art of battle." The democracies were tired, old, and tied to the earth, they said. They would be swept into the garbage pail of history.

The shape of the Second World War was becoming clear long before the "main event." Airplanes helped Italy destroy Ethiopia, the oldest independent country in

East Africa. In 1935, dictator Benito Mussolini's ground troops in Ethiopia were supplied by parachute drops of live cattle and goats. His dive-bombers killed many of the poorly armed tribesmen. Vittorio Mussolini, his son, wrote poems about what it felt like to drop bombs on a crowd of Ethiopians. The crowd opened up like a giant red rose; "It was so entertaining," said he.

This was only the beginning of the air terror. In 1937, the Japanese invaded China and bombed its crowded cities. During the Spanish Civil War, 1936–1939, the Spanish dictator, General Francisco Franco's planes bombed Madrid, Barcelona, and other cities. Then on April 26, 1937, the German Condor Legion, which Hitler had sent to help a brother dictator, bombed the small town of Guernica.

There had never been anything like it before. Guernica was not a military base; it was undefended. Guernica could not harm Franco in any way. Attacking it was to be an "experiment," its people human guinea pigs. For the Condor Legion was already in training for the larger war Hitler was planning and certain things had to be studied. Exactly how much damage would an air attack do to a built-up area? What sort of bombs were best? Would machine-gunning the place when the bombers finished do much more damage? How much? And so General Wolfram von Richthofen (cousin of the "Red Baron" of the First World War) ordered Guernica bombed "without regard to the civilian population." And bombed it was, and strafed by low-flying planes. And what a victory for Nazi "science!" Out of seven thousand Guernicans, three thousand were killed or wounded.

War was coming to Europe again, and sooner or later the United States would have to fight in it. The best we had in the 1930s was a "fifth-rate air force," as one general called it. The German air force could have had our 500 first-class warplanes for breakfast and flown away hungry.

President Franklin D. Roosevelt (FDR) seemed the last person on earth to support air power. He loved ships. He loved sailing them, loved building models of them, loved spending endless hours looking at them. Even today the first thing the visitor to his Hyde Park, New York, home notices are the framed pictures of every type of ship. He had been Assistant Secretary of the Navy in the First World War, and did not like the way Billy Mitchell sank big battleships with tiny planes of wood, and wire, and canvas, but he learned the lesson of Guernica.

In September, 1938, FDR called his military advisors to the White House. Hap Arnold was there and told what happened. He could tell from the President's voice and manner that he was upset. Peace was slipping away and there was no telling how much time the country had to make up for past mistakes. Then came the clincher. The commander in chief looked each visitor in the eye and said in that rich voice of his: "I want airplanes — now — and lots of them."

FDR had spoken none too soon, for almost a year to the day after this meeting Hitler's planes and tanks sliced into Poland. Britain and France declared war on Germany and the Second World War began. No one could have known then what we know now: it would be the most terrible war in history.

Poland fell in a month, September, 1939. In May, 1940, Hitler's war machine turned west, crushing Holland and Belgium. It smashed across the French border and kept going. The spring was mild, the sun shining brightly as German troops decorated their helmets with red poppies from the fields and sang gay songs as they sped toward Paris. The French surrendered, leaving the British to rescue what was left of the Allied armies, two hundred fifty thousand men, from the Dunkirk, France, beaches before the Germans could close in for the kill.

FDR's calls for planes and more planes grew louder, but not even he could wave a magic wand to give the country what it needed. Much had to be done quickly and at the same time.

First there were the planes. The United States aircraft industry in 1940 was not prepared to build thousands of planes a year; FDR wanted ten thousand by the end of 1940, another twenty thousand in 1941. Unlike the auto industry, it had not gone in for mass production and interchangeable parts. Its factories were designed to make small numbers of high-quality airliners and private planes. When an order for twenty or thirty planes of a certain type came in, the parts were run off in small "job

Tom Woodburn's recruiting poster was drawn in 1939, soon after President Roosevelt said he wanted planes, "and lots of them." The planes shown are P-35 fighters, which were outdated even when they were used for the first time in combat during the Japanese invasion of the Philippines shortly after Pearl Harbor.

lots," just enough for the job at hand. Little was done to save time by dividing the assembly of these parts into many short, easy steps. The parts were simply gathered in one place and put together from the ground up by skilled mechanics who were proud of everything they made.

Government orders changed everything. The United States had to meet not only its own military needs but those of Great Britain as well. After Dunkirk the British stood alone against Hitler's Third Reich. Had they not been able to buy American-made weapons on easy credit terms called Lend-Lease, they might have gone under.

American energy and know-how were tested and came through with flying colors. Old aircraft factories had their insides torn out and modernized. New factories sprang up almost overnight where there had been corn-fields. Everywhere mass production and assembly-line methods became the rule. Each operation in putting together a warplane was broken down into its smallest part. Workers waited at hundreds of stations along the moving assembly line, and each knew only how to do the simple job for which he or she had been trained.

Wings, tails, and fuselage sections were welded and riveted in the parts plants. At the engine plants, bolts, screws, cylinders and countless other parts were put together and tested. But the main work took place in the assembly plants, where giant overhead cranes brought the fuselage to a station to have the wings attached. Something else was added at each station along the assembly line: engines, wiring, superchargers, wingtips, flaps, de-icers, turrets, propellers, armor plates, landing gear, wheels, tires. When the plane rolled off at the end of the line it was inspected, gassed up, and test flown. Only when it passed the test did the Air Force man on the scene accept it for the service.

The aircraft plants could never have run without women. As the need for planes grew, and as the draft took more men for the armed forces, women filled in for them on the assembly lines. They took their work seriously, because soon their menfolk might be meeting the enemy in those planes. Soon the whole country was singing about its new sweetheart, *"Rosie the Riveter."* Dressed in overalls and a plaid blouse, her hair covered with a bright kerchief, she stood there under a bomber's wing, her rivet gun going *RAT-TAT-TAT-A-TAT*. Rosie, her sisters and her brothers, built nearly three hundred thousand military planes between July 1, 1940, and August 31, 1945, at a cost of $45 billion.

But planes cannot fly themselves, or fix themselves, or defend themselves in battle. People do these things, and men enlisted, first in the thousands and then in the millions. The Army Air Force went from 23,453 in 1939, to 2,372,293 in the peak year 1944.

New ways had to be found to train so many men. The Air Force called in psychologists to prepare tests of different abilities: mathematics, mechanical skills, quick reflexes, clear thinking under pressure. Recruits were given these tests to find the best person for each job. Only then were men chosen for pilot training or to become navigators, radio operators, and so on.

Women also played an important role in building the new Air Force. Hundreds of young women who had learned to fly before the war joined the WASPs (Women's Airforce Service Pilots). In addition to ferrying warplanes to bases in the United States and overseas, women had top security clearances as military coders and decoders.

Meanwhile planners were deciding how the nation's growing air strength should be used. The first four of the numbered air forces were formed in March, 1941. The First, Second, Third, and Fourth Air Force were stationed in the U.S. to train airmen and defend our shores. Early

the next month, American and British staff officers held a secret meeting in Washington. They decided that the United States should beef up its air units in Hawaii and the Philippine Islands in case Japan attacked or came into the war on Germany's side.

Mass production in the "Arsenal of Democracy." B-24 Liberator bombers on the assembly line at General Dynamics' Fort Worth Division plant. This factory extends back as far as the eye can see.

This buildup was not completed as planned. Some B-17 bombers had already arrived from the West Coast and others were still in the air when it happened as Billy Mitchell said it would — at Pearl Harbor "on a fine, quiet Sunday morning."

At 2:26, Eastern Standard Time, station WOR interrupted its broadcast of the Giant-Dodger football game from the Polo Grounds in New York. FLASH: "PEARL HARBOR HAS BEEN BOMBED BY THE JAPANESE!"

The date was December 7, 1941. Time had run out.

2

The Yanks are Coming

Winston S. Churchill was stepping out of the bathtub, naked as the day he was born. Just then the door of his guest room in the White House burst open and an aide wheeled in FDR; the crippled President always used a wheelchair at home. Embarrassed, FDR apologized for not knocking. The dripping Churchill smiled and said: "The prime minister of Great Britain has nothing to conceal from the president of the United States."

The two leaders were good friends, but they were also allies. The prime minister had not come all this way to pay a social call. It was less than two weeks since the attack of Pearl Harbor and he was leading a high-level British team to a meeting in Washington. Code-named ARCADIA, this meeting lasted from December 20, 1941, to January 24, 1942. Its aim was to draw up the main

Allied plan for fighting the Second World War. Such planning was needed now, especially since Hitler had declared war on the United States on December 11.

The Allied leaders decided at ARCADIA that they should not divide their forces equally. True, they were fighting two wars, one in Europe the other in the Pacific and Asia. But Hitler's Germany was the stronger enemy and the most dangerous. Already the man Germans called *Der Führer* (the Chief) was master of Western Europe. His tanks stood at the gates of Moscow in the east, while Field Marshal Erwin Rommel, the "Desert Fox," was advancing in North Africa. Japan would have to wait until the Allies defeated the Nazis. Until then, Europe had first call on America's men and resources.

It was also decided at ARCADIA that air power would play a key part in defeating Germany. The big question was: How should this key be used?

There were two main ideas about using air power: *tactical* versus *strategic*. "Tactical" means using a weapon to win battles by defeating the opposing armies. "Strategic" means using it to win wars by destroying the enemy's ability to fight. The Germans believed in using airplanes tactically, the Allies in using them strategically.

These ideas owed much to each side's experiences during the First World War. The Germans' plan in 1914 depended upon speed. Their armies were supposed to cut through Belgium, capture Paris, and win the war in a few weeks. They didn't. Instead they bogged down in fifty-one months of trench warfare. The armies dug in along a thousand-mile front and slugged it out with artillery and poison gas. Sometimes thousands of men charged across the "no man's land" that separated the trench lines. Usually they were driven back with heavy losses. Millions of men died, but still the Germans couldn't break through. Slowly the Allies, joined by the United States, put on the pressure until Germany had to give up.

Lesson: German armies must move faster in the next war. They must move *through* the enemy and *over* him. They must use the tank and airplane to make *"Blitzkrieg,"* a German word meaning "lightning war."

When Hitler came to power in 1933, he asked Hermann Goering to help him build a modern war machine. You'd never know by looking at him that Goering had any special skills — except, that is, a skill for making himself look silly. He liked taking drugs, wearing flashy clothes, and overeating. *"Der Dicke"* (Fat One) wore perfume and had his face made up with rouge.

Yet Goering was more dangerous than he looked. The Fat One had another nickname that he also deserved. "Iron Man," they called him. He knew everything there was to know about airplanes. He knew how to build them, how to fly them, and how to fight in them. A famous pilot himself, he had taken over the "Flying Circus" when the Red Baron was shot down.

Hitler wanted Goering to build his new air force, the Luftwaffe. He worked hard, and before long Germany had the most powerful air force in Europe, maybe the world.

Germany's "air weapon" — for that's what *Luftwaffe* means—was not supposed to wear down an enemy over many months of fighting. Nor was it a weapon of defense. No, it was a weapon of attack, a weapon for bringing victory quickly. With it the Germans hoped to destroy enemy armies before they could begin to fight back.

The Luftwaffe started the Second World War with over a half-million men and three thousand warplanes. Its planes were of three kinds. First came the twin-engined bombers; these could not travel very far, but were fast and could work closely with ground troops. Then there were the dive-bombers, especially the Junkers JU-87 Stuka. This plane even looked nasty. Its jawlike radiator and clawlike landing gear made it look like a swooping

Partners in crime. Adolf Hitler, dictator of Germany, with Reich Marshal Hermann Goering, head of the Luftwaffe, and Field Marshal Wilhelm Keitel, chief of the German Army High Command.

vulture. Sirens fitted to its wingtips gave off horrible screams when it dived, scaring even the best soldiers.

For years Germany's fighters ruled the skies over Europe. The Messerschmitt ME-109 was fast, easy to fly, and armed with machine guns and cannon. But even it was no match for the Focke-Wulf FW-190. Introduced in 1941, this was the best all-around fighter of its time. The Germans called it *Wuerger* — "Butcher Bird." It could do whatever the ME-109 could do, only do more of it and do it faster. British and American bomber pilots knew that its guns could destroy a plane many times its own size.

The only type of plane the Luftwaffe didn't have was the long-range, four-engined, heavy bomber. The Germans didn't want to build such a plane. Hitler and Goering decided not to waste scarce raw materials and labor on big bombers when the *Blitzkrieg* would defeat Germany's enemies so easily.

The formula for *Blitzkrieg* was simple and deadly: hit the enemy first; hit him hard; and keep on hitting him until he surrendered. The Germans tried never to let an enemy know he was going to be attacked until the moment the bombs began to fall. This meant beginning a war without bothering to declare it. The Luftwaffe simply appeared over the enemy's airfields and destroyed his planes on the ground. The few that escaped were easily shot down.

Bombers then ranged far behind the lines, tearing up enemy communications and preventing reinforcements from reaching the front. Light forces — motorcycle troops, motorized cannon, armored cars, small tanks —

Junkers JU-87 Stuka dive bomber. This plane was useful against tanks and for giving close infantry support in the early days of the war. But it was no match for the British Spitfire and the American fast fighters. The low-slung radiator, gull-wings, and wheel-guards made it look like an ugly bird of prey.

sped into enemy territory. They used the Stukas as a kind of flying artillery. Whenever they ran into trouble or needed pinpoint hits, they radioed for an "air strike." Finally heavy tanks followed by foot soldiers enlarged the pocket, mopped up, and regrouped for the next advance, all under an umbrella of Luftwaffe fighters.

Blitzkrieg worked beautifully until the tanks pulled up to the English Channel. Then they stopped short, for tank columns cannot ride on water. The Nazi war machine had come to a deeper and a wider "trench" than anything seen in the First World War.

Goering knew that he had to wipe out the Royal Air

Force (RAF) before an invasion could begin. As long as the British had enough warplanes they could chop up any fleet that tried to cross the Channel. Worse, they could cover the Royal Navy, allowing it to attack the German fleet as it gathered in Dutch and French ports.

But without big bombers the Luftwaffe couldn't reach many RAF bases or the factories that built its planes. Even if twin-engined bombers could reach these targets, their fighter escorts could not, and bombers without escorts are sitting ducks. As good as the ME-109 was, it couldn't carry enough fuel to go with the bombers *and* tangle with RAF Fighter Command's Spitfires and Hurricanes. Both were short-range planes, but very fast, strong, and piloted by men whose homes were below.

As it did for the Germans, the experience of the First World War helps explain how the British decided to fight the Second. They too promised never to repeat the tragedy of the trenches, in which over a million of their best young men died in battles that led nowhere. Britain is a small country and cannot easily make up such heavy losses.

Lesson: in the next war Britain must move slowly. She must fight "economically," making sure to do so, not with huge land armies, but from a distance with airplanes. Let machines take the place of men. Play for time. Stand off, safe behind the English Channel, and smash the enemy with bombers until he broke or grew tired of fighting.

The British idea of using air power strategically grew out of a better understanding of modern war than the Nazi leaders'. Gone were the days when armies could advance far from home and live off the countryside they passed through. Victory in the twentieth century depended as much on what happened on the "home front" as on the fighting front. The roots of modern armies and navies go back thousands of miles to the factories of the homeland. Cut these roots and the bravest soldiers must surrender or be killed. Without gun factories there could be no guns; it was that simple.

Sir Arthur Harris, head of RAF Bomber Command, was a British Billy Mitchell. Like Mitchell, "Bomber Harris" made enemies easily, only he made them by using a softer voice. And like Mitchell he believed airplanes could win wars all by themselves.

By the beginning of 1942, British factories were sending Harris large numbers of new types of heavy bombers. The Halifax, Sterling, and Lancaster bombers were slow, clumsy monsters with few guns and little armor plate to protect the crew. They were really trucks with wings. They could fly to the heart of Germany and dump as much as seven tons of high explosives per plane. They needed no fighter cover, because their cover was the darkness of night.

Harris knew that bombing factories by moonlight or through an overcast was inaccurate. It was a safe bet that in most cases the bombers would hit everything *except* the factory they were aiming for. All right, then, Harris thought. If the RAF couldn't hit a barn door at night then let it aim for the whole barn. In other words, aim for the whole town in which a factory is located instead of the factory itself.

"Area bombing," as Harris's idea was called, might not destroy machines but it would surely hurt the people who ran them. Harris felt hurting, even killing, civilians was a correct way to make war. After all, civilians are warriors anyhow—warriors of the home front. The German people supported the lunatic Hitler and worked for him. They should be made to pay the price for his war.

Harris liked to do things in a big way. On the night of May 30, 1942, he began Operation MILLENNIUM. The name comes from the Latin word for "thousand," and MILLENNIUM was the first thousand-plane air raid in history. The target was Cologne, a chemical and synthetic rubber center on the Rhine River. Compared to what happened later, the 469 people killed that night were few. But nothing like it had ever happened before, and the raid upset the Nazi leaders.

Goering used to boast that no enemy aircraft would ever enter Germany; if they did, he said, "You can call me Meier." Meier is a Jewish name, and the Nazis hated Jews. They murdered six million innocent Jews during the Holocaust of 1939–1945. And so Goering put a lot on the line when he made his boast. For if he failed, the German people were invited to laugh him out of office. Cologne made them laugh, only their laughter had a sharp edge to it. Jokes about "Mister Meier" and "Meier's hunting horns" (air raid sirens) became popular in the bomb shelters.

Neither Goering nor Hitler laughed about Cologne. When told of the bombing Goering refused to believe the news. "Impossible," he shouted, "that many bombs cannot be dropped in a single night." Then he ordered a report with the "correct" damage figures sent to Hitler.

Der Führer already knew the truth. When an aide of Goering's reported the false damage figures, Hitler lost his temper. He screamed that the Luftwaffe had betrayed Germany and lied to him. When Goering came to headquarters later that day, Hitler refused to shake his hand, but left him standing in the doorway with his outstretched hand in the air. Goering was upset, for the man he worshipped as a god no longer trusted him. From then on Hitler wouldn't listen to Goering even when he gave good advice. *That* was good for the Allies.

Cologne was bad, but what the RAF did to Hamburg was like the crack of doom. Germany's second city, next only to Berlin, Hamburg lies on the Elbe River a little way inland from the North Sea. Its docks and factories were very important to the German war effort, and the RAF wanted them destroyed. After dropping leaflets warning people to leave the city, on five nights between July 24, and August 3, 1943, the RAF carried out Operation GOMORRAH. (The Bible tells how God drowned the city of Gomorrah in fire and brimstone for its sins.)

The RAF made the first "fire storm" in history in Hamburg. The high explosives and fire bombs that rained down on the city started thousands of fires. There were so many fires that the city's fire department couldn't get to them all. These fires soon joined into a single thundering blaze. As the hot air rose faster and faster, it created a vacuum at ground level, pulling in cool air from outside the city. The fresh air made the fire even hotter, creating winds that shot through the city like a blowtorch. The glow of Hamburg's fires could be seen from 120 miles away. At least thirty-seven thousand five hundred of its people lost their lives and a million others were left homeless.

Hitler had promised to make Germany's cities the envy of the world. But now, when the going became rough, he never visited Hamburg or any of the other bombed places. Whenever his private train passed through them, servants pulled down the shades to spare him the ugly sights.

The United States Army Air Force's (USAAF's) idea of strategic bombing differed from the RAF's. Its officers had been taught that bombing war plants with the workers in them was one thing, but attacking people in their homes for the sake of hurting them was immoral. As a 1926 training book explained: "It is wrong to send planes simply to drop bombs over a large area."

General Arnold believed in pinpoint attacks on the enemy's military, government, and industrial centers. The effects of such attacks, he said, would soon travel through the enemy's entire country, paralyzing its ability to make war.

The USAAF needed a special plane to do the kind of job he had in mind. The British bombers were big but too slow; the German bombers were fast but couldn't travel far enough or carry enough bombs. The perfect bomber, Arnold said, should be able to fly high, fly fast, and fly far. It should be able to fly to a target in broad daylight and drop tons of bombs "into a pickle barrel" from thirty thousand feet. Sheets of plate armor in the crew areas, plus plenty of heavy machine guns, should allow it to smash through any opposition and defend itself without fighter escorts.

By the time of Pearl Harbor, the USAAF had two heavyweights to throw into battle: the B-17 and B-24. Hitler was right to boast that he had built a wall of steel around his *Festung Europa,* his Fortress Europe. FDR was also right in reminding him that he had forgotten to put a roof over it.

The Boeing Airplane Company began work on the B-17 in 1934, and after many changes, its "G" model became the favorite of U.S. airmen in Europe. It was powered by four supercharged 4,800-horsepower Wright Cyclone engines. An airplane engine is like an automobile engine: it must mix air with gasoline so that the fuel can turn to vapor and explode, providing the power to drive the vehicle. Since the air becomes thinner higher up, a greater amount of air must be forced into a high-flying bomber's motors. The supercharger, which was first widely used in American heavy bombers, let the Cyclones gulp as much air as they needed.

The Cyclones drove the B-17 at a top speed of 287 miles an hour at twenty-five thousand feet; it flew a little slower at thirty-five thousand feet, its highest altitude. When loaded with five thousand pounds of bombs, it had a combat radius of 700 miles. *"Combat radius"* is the longest distance a plane can travel from its base to a target and back along a straight line. If we take London, England, as the starting point, the B-17 could sweep a 700-mile arc covering every important target in Germany and occupied Western Europe.

The B-17 deserved its nickname, "Flying Fortress." It bristled with as many as thirteen heavy machine guns

Pilot and copilot had their hands full flying the B-17.
A cockpit view, showing the steering columns and maze
of controls and dials.

placed to defend it against fighters coming in from every angle.

If ever fighting men loved a fighting machine, that machine was the Flying Fortress. She was a real beauty, a "queen" with tapered 104-foot wings, slim, rounded seventy-five-foot fuselage, and towering nineteen-foot tail. The engineers had made her a marvelously steady plane, instantly obeying the slightest touch on the controls.

And she was "rugged," a word airmen did not use often. Crews felt safer in a B-17 than in any other bomber of the day. Although her metal skin was so thin that you could jab a screwdriver through it, she could take a lot of punishment and still keep flying. But the wear and tear of combat was so great that by 1944, even the Flying Fortress had an average life of 231 *days,* during which it might fly twenty-one missions. No wonder factories worked every minute of every day to manufacture more planes.

The Consolidated Aircraft Company started its B-24 project in 1939, almost as soon as FDR gave the go-ahead for a large air force. Like the Flying Fortress, the "Liberator" had a ten-man crew — pilot, copilot, bombardier, radioman, navigator, flight engineer, tail gunner, ball turret gunner, two waist gunners — and plenty of machine guns. But the B-24 was faster, had a longer range, and carried a heavier bomb load than the older plane. It traveled over three hundred miles an hour with eighty-five hundred pounds of bombs, although it wasn't as steady as the B-17 or able to shake off battle damage as easily.

The Eighth Air Force was the spearhead of the American attack on Hitler's empire.* The first commander of the "Mighty Eighth" was Major General Carl A. Spaatz. At fifty-one, the veteran World War I flyer still had the best of his career ahead of him. Before long "Tooey," as everyone called him, would take charge of all United States Strategic Air Forces in Europe, then in the Pacific, the only officer to hold such high command in both war zones.

Tooey knew the score in Europe. He had gone to Britain in the dark days after Dunkirk as an observer. He saw the Battle of Britain, saw the dogfights and the bombings of London, firsthand. He came to admire the cool courage and ability of the RAF leaders. And they came to like him, his impish sense of humor, his way of calming a tense situation with a joke. Asked to sign the guest book at an RAF base, he wrote the word "Spy!" Once his hosts got over their shock, everyone had a good laugh and was able to relax.

Spaatz's assistant and head of Eighth Bomber Command was Brigadier General Ira C. Eaker. At forty-six, Eaker had grown up with Army aviation. He admired

* There were nine combat air forces during the Second World War. The Sixth and Eleventh served in the Panama Canal Zone and Alaska. The Eighth operated from the British Isles. Based in the Mediterranean region and North Africa were the Ninth, Twelfth, and Fifteenth. The Fifth, Seventh, Tenth, Thirteenth, and Fourteenth covered the Pacific and China-Burma-India areas. The Twentieth was formed in 1945, for the B-29s bombing Japan from the Marianas.

General Arnold, having helped him with the writing of books on flying: *This Flying Game* (1936) and *Winged Warfare* (1941). A few days after ARCADIA, Arnold ordered him to England to make arrangements for the coming USAAF bomber offensive.

Eaker and his small staff had plenty to do when they arrived in April, 1942. Setting up headquarters was a good place to begin, and Eighth Bomber Command soon found a home in Wycombe Abbey, a beautiful

General Henry H. (Hap) Arnold, chief of the Army Air Force, chats with Major General Ira C. Eaker, chief of Eighth Bomber Command and later commander of the Eighth Air Force in England.

building that used to house a boarding school for wealthy girls. It was located at High Wycombe, thirty miles west of London and less than five miles from RAF Bomber Command headquarters.

Here at High Wycombe, code-named PINETREE, the Americans had countless meetings with RAF officers. Day in and day out, often until three or four o'clock in the morning, they went over the thousands of details necessary for bringing a whole air force across the Atlantic Ocean and getting it ready for battle. Airfield assignments and cod liver pills, intelligence staffs and typists, military police and laundry service, antiaircraft protection and mud control: every question had to be discussed, settled, and put in the form of a written order. *Everything* in the military takes the form of a written order.

The British were good hosts, making the Yanks feel welcome. "Tell us what you want," the British chiefs said, "and if we have it, it is yours." Like the friends they were, they gave whatever was asked without letting on that they had to do without because the thing requested was in short supply.

As busy as things were behind the scenes, everything was perfectly calm in public. At a banquet given in Eaker's honor in June by the Lord Mayor of High Wycombe, he answered welcoming speeches in just twenty-three words: "We won't do much talking until we've done more fighting. We hope that when we leave, you'll be glad we came. Thank you." Then he sat down.

There could be no fighting without airfields. The Eighth took over 127 RAF bomber fields, plus all the buildings and shops needed to service planes and to house ground crews. Most airfields were located in East Anglia, a region of farms and small towns northeast of London.

Those members of the Eighth who worked on the ground arrived aboard the liner *Queen Elizabeth* in June. The planes came separately, flown across the Atlantic by their own crews. Although the flight was long, over thirty-five hundred miles altogether, few planes were lost. Some were "pranged," or cracked up, during landings on slippery runways. Others had engine trouble and came down on icecaps or ditched at sea. A few were sent off course by false compass bearings radioed by the Germans, crashing when their fuel ran out.

Yet nearly all crewmen survived, sometimes under awful conditions. One Flying Fortress crash-landed on the Greenland icecap. (In spite of its name, Greenland is not green, but a desert of bluish-white ice.) The crew cut off the blades of a twisted propeller with a hacksaw and used the engine to warm the cabin and power the radio generator. They were rescued a few days later by a Navy flying boat.

A notation dated July 4, 1942, appears in Eighth Bomber Command's roster book: *"Arrival of aircraft: 1 B-17E. Total: 1."* This plane was the first of a stream that would flow with growing force until Hitler's Germany had been crushed.

The B-17s did not make our first attack on Fortress Europe. For on the day that lone plane arrived, six crews under Captain Charles C. Kegelman borrowed American-built A-20 "Boston" light bombers from the RAF and joined six of its crews for a raid on Luftwaffe bases in Holland. What better way could there be of celebrating the 166th year of American independence?

The raid was not a military success. Two of the American crews failed to locate the target and returned with their bombs; two were shot down; and two dropped their bombs, causing little damage. But Captain Kegelman surprised everyone, himself included. With one engine burning, he bounced his ship off the ground, turned his guns on an enemy position, and flew away. Kegelman had been a good messenger, delivering the Eighth's "calling card" to the Jerries (a nickname for the German forces).

The first B-17s went into action a month later, on August 7. General Eaker himself led eighteen planes against railroad yards at Rouen, France. Little damage was done and all planes returned safely. One Flying Fortress, though, nearly didn't make it. It was almost brought down, not by German guns but by a flock of pigeons. The birds broke through the plexiglass nose and "slightly damaged" the navigator and bombardier, according to the official report.

Eaker was taking things slowly, not wanting to send his crews on big missions until they had more combat experience. He lay low after Rouen, sending out only a few sorties at a time against easy targets. A "sortie" is a single mission by a single plane.

On October 9, he ordered 108 Flying Fortresses and Liberators to bomb the steel mills at Lille, France. Lille was special for two reasons. It was the first time the Eighth had sent a large number of planes to a single target. That alone taught valuable lessons, especially about controlling traffic over the target, which at Lille looked like the roads around Boston on a holiday week-end. Also for the first time the term "air raid" didn't fit. A raid of a quick jab and withdrawal by a small force. Lille was a pitched *battle* fought high above the earth. Only three planes were lost, but the action was so sharp that the airmen were shaken up by their experience. This war, they decided, was not going to be easy. As soon as the crew of *Helzapoppin* landed their battered ship they changed its name to *Borrowed Time*.

The feeling of living on borrowed time grew stronger when the Eighth learned that one of its targets would be the German navy. All along the French coast on the Bay of Biscay the enemy had built a network of submarine bases. The U-boats operating from these bases were sinking thousands of tons of Allied shipping each month. If the sinkings continued, they might be able to knock the Eighth out of the war without shooting down a single plane. For all the Eighth's fuel was carried in tanker ships up the Thames River and unloaded into pipelines leading to the East Anglican airfields.

Throughout the winter of 1942, the Eighth pounded the U-boat bases. It was not a pleasant assignment and most of the time the bombers did no damage at all. Submarines are housed in low concrete boxes called "pens." Each German U-boat pen was capped with twenty feet of solid concrete reinforced with steel bars.

U-boat pens are small, especially when you are looking down on them from five miles above the earth. If the Flying Fortress crews wanted to hit them squarely, they had to drop their bombs from seventy-five hundred feet or lower. The B-17 is a big plane, and from that altitude it is an easy target for antiaircraft gunners. Things became so hot that the bomber men called St. Nazaire "Flak City," but that name could have fit any of the other towns the Germans used for submarine bases. Many planes were shot down, yet the crews knew that even if they placed their bombs right on target the submarines remained safe in their concrete and steel shells.

This was not the widespread destruction General Arnold and the other big-bomber people had promised. The American taxpayer was spending lots of money to raise clouds of dust over U-boat pens. The Eighth's record was very sorry indeed. The Nazi leaders feared the RAF because it was burning their cities every night. They laughed at the American daytime raids. Why should they have been afraid when the Eighth had been in the war for a full year and still hadn't dropped a bomb on Germany itself. Bombs dropped on French or Dutch towns actually helped the Germans, since the people there blamed the Allied airmen for their troubles.

The Luftwaffe began to drop nasty messages on Eighth airfields. "Where are the American bombers?" they asked. Goering scorned American claims that its factories were building thousands of warplanes a month. "The Americans do very well in some technical fields," he said. "We know they produce a colossal number of fast cars. And the development of radio is one of their special achievements, and so is the razor blade. But you must not forget, there is one word in their language that is written with a capital B and this word is Bluff."

The winter of 1942 was a low point for the Eighth. Men and machines were trickling away, lost in attacks of little value. Living conditions in England were almost as bad for morale as battle losses. Military airfields are not built for comfort but for easy defense. In England they were flat, grassy plains that stretched two miles on each side. At the center of the plain two concrete ribbons, the runways, crossed. A paved track called the "perimeter taxiway" circled the field. The bombers moved along this track before taxiing onto the runways for takeoff. Hangars, office buildings, machine shops, mess halls, and barracks were scattered around the area far away from each other; the idea was not to give the enemy an easy target by having everything close together.

Americans never got used to the English climate and the English mud. The bomber bases were often "socked-in" by fog for weeks. Men became moody and short-tempered in the gloom. The damp cold got into everything, and there was no way to make the barracks comfortable, as coal was scarce in England too.

Mud was everywhere; gooey, sloppy mud that sucked the galoshes off men's feet. Passing trucks and jeeps splattered pedestrians from head to toe. Mud oozed onto the runways and splattered the planes' plexiglass as they took off, freezing solid and interfering with the bombardiers' visibility. Bombs and lives were wasted because of those muddy smudges.

The whole daylight bombing program was in danger during that winter of 1942. The RAF had little faith in it or in the plane the Americans were using to carry it out. For once they agreed with Dr. Josef Goebbels, Nazi propaganda minister. While Goebbels called the B-17s "Flying Coffins," RAF men named them "Flying Targets."

The B-17's bomb load was so small, compared to

the Lancaster's, that the RAF handed over its few Flying Fortresses to Coastal Command for long-range antisubmarine patrols. Air Marshal Harris even suggested the daylight bombing be scrapped and the American planes turned over to the RAF's night offensive. He once told Eaker: "We have to use saturation bombing. We kill lots of workmen, true, but may I remind you, when you destroy a fighter factory it takes the Germans six weeks to replace it. When I kill a workman it takes twenty-five years to replace him."

The question of day versus night bombing was settled early the following year. Churchill, FDR, and their military advisors met in Casablanca, Morocco, in January, 1943, to plan their next moves. North Africa had just been liberated by a United States-British army and the leaders decided to move on from there to the island of Sicily and then to invade Italy. Operation OVERLORD, the invasion of France, would come in 1944. They gave Germany the choice of "unconditional surrender" or total destruction.

But what about the bomber offensive? Here there was disagreement. Churchill plainly said that he was disappointed with the Eighth. When the right moment came he would ask his friend FDR to lump its operations together with those of the RAF.

Eaker and the prime minister met three days after Eaker arrived in Casablanca. Churchill was friendly, reminding the general that he liked Americans; his own mother had been American. But he stuck to his guns. Daylight bombing was a mistake and ought to be ended.

Eaker replied with clear, well-reasoned arguments.

These arguments boiled down to the fact that daylight bombing was more accurate and used fewer planes than the RAF's night attacks. Each force should fight the way it knew best without interfering with the other. That way "bombing around the clock" would keep the Germans busy twenty-four hours a day.

Churchill was convinced. He especially liked the phrase "bombing around the clock." Eaker remembers that the Prime Minister repeated it several times under his breath as if he was tasting it. Then he said: *"Bomb the devil round the clock."* And that's what he told the British government when he returned home. The new USAAF-RAF air offensive was about to begin.

Before the Casablanca conference ended, the Allied leaders issued an order known as the Casablanca Directive. Their air staffs were to work out plans for "the progressive destruction and dislocation of the German military, industrial, and economic system and the undermining of the morale of the German people to the point where capacity for armed resistance is fatally weakened." In other words, the full weight of Allied air power was to fall on Germany's ability to make war.

Two days after the leaders flew home from Casablanca, January 26, 1943, the word was flashed to the muddy bomber bases in England: "The target for today is Germany."

3

A Mission Over Target Germany

Let's invite ourselves along on an Eighth Air Force bombing mission "somewhere over Germany." It is 1615 hours and we are at the Daily Operations Conference at PINETREE. The meeting room is better protected than any U-boat pen, buried beneath thirty feet of steel and concrete. There is nothing cheerful about the large square room, nothing to show that it is anything but a place to plan destruction.

There are five officers in the room: the chief of Eighth's bomber forces and his aides. Each is an expert in some area of mission planning. Thick folders of papers, maps, photos, messages, and scribbled notes are scattered on the table in front of them.

The only really colorful thing in the room is the wall map of Europe, and this is anything but cheerful. It is downright depressing. For the map is laced with wide red lines, the aerial routes to and from targets in Germany and occupied Europe. These lines are called "the blood highways of the air." They deserve the name.

The officers are choosing tomorrow morning's target. They have to consider everything in making their choice.

What Luftwaffe squadrons are based along the bomber's route? If it's the Abbeville Kids, Goering's favorite squadrons, our boys will have a bad time.

How near can our fighters escort us to the target? And how many fighters can we count on? A couple of hundred would do just fine.

How much antiaircraft fire can we expect from ground batteries?

What size bombs should we use? High explosive or incendiary?

Will the weather hold? How much cloud cover will there be over the target if that cold front moves in from the north?

After three hours of this sort of questioning back and forth, the chief decides. The final responsibility is his alone, and he takes it seriously. For every command decision finally boils down to people's lives.

Eighth Bomber Command is made up of units that become smaller as they get further from the top. Just below command headquarters are three air divisions, each led by a general. Air divisions are made up of four combat wings apiece, the wing being the largest force an officer, usually a colonel, can control in battle. The wing has three bombardment groups of four squadrons each. The squadron is the basic air unit, having twelve planes, 120 airmen.

It is 1900 hours when headquarters issues the warning order alerting the air divisions that a "show" is coming up. Immediately teletype machines in their communications centers begin to clatter and cough out long ribbons of paper.

Although the flight crews haven't been told anything yet, they know that a mission is in the works. They've seen the low trailers shuttling back and forth from the bomb dumps with full loads. The roads around many a country village are lined on both sides with neatly stacked layers of bombs. Any child on a bicycle knows they're there, but the Germans don't because they are covered with branches and sheets of artificial grass.

Darkness is falling as the trailers race along the narrow country lanes. Sometimes they turn a corner too sharply, flinging a couple of 500-pounders into the mud. No problem; they will not explode as long as their fuses are somewhere else.

At 1930 hours the loudspeakers break into the card games at the canteen, ordering certain crews from certain squadrons and groups to "hit the sack" early.

There are many tired men who aren't able to go to bed. At 2200 hours the teletypes at First Air Division headquarters start clattering again: the field order is coming through. This outlines the mission, leaving it to the division's planners to fill in the details. Further down the line at the combat wing level they will refine things still further. Finally the teletypes will sound in the group message centers. Now everything that command has planned, that air division and combat wing have worked out, will be put into operation.

Time: 0200 on the new day. S-2, our group intelligence officer, is snoring like an Atlantic storm when the duty sergeant shakes his shoulder. While S-2 rubs the sleep from his eyes the group commander, group navigator, group flak officer, cooks, and motor pool drivers are tumbling out of the sack.

Each officer hurries to his place in the operations room. This is a world of its own. Behind its airtight, gas-proof doors and double blackout curtains, the lights are burning brightly.

The group commander sits at his desk with the field order, studying every detail, making notes, and memorizing key parts. The morning's timetable is set: wake up the crews at 0400; breakfast at 0430; briefing at 0500; takeoff at 0630, one plane every fifteen seconds.

Tension mounts as the work goes on. Officers pin large sheets of clear plastic over the wall maps, then with grease pencils they rule long lines: the red lines are the pathway to the target, the black lines lead home.

S-2 leans over the target chart. On it he enters the IP (Initial Point) where the planes will turn toward the target; the AP (Aiming Point) where the bombardier takes control of the aircraft; and the MPI (Median Point of Impact), or bull's-eye where the bombs will land.

The flak officer is studying blowups of aerial photographs. This morning he has perfect pictures. He is checking every feature of the land along the bombers' course, circling the antiaircraft positions in red.

Cameras and picture-taking methods made great advances during the Second World War. Large wide-angle lenses made it possible to piece together hundreds of overlapping pictures to create a photo-map of a whole region. Powerful flash bombs lit miles of land and water for night photography. Special B-24s called "flying dark rooms" had their own developing equipment and staffs of photo-interpretors who radioed important information quickly.

Nearby the group flying officer is working out the takeoff and assembly procedures. He is an important person, more important in certain ways than the commander himself. For it is he who gives each plane its place in the formation, and where a plane is in that formation has a lot to do with whether or not it returns in one piece.

At 0400 the duty sergeant turns on the barracks' lights. Somehow everyone slips into their clothes. Moments later they're outside staggering toward the mess hall.

Through the darkness the airmen can make out massive shapes: planes. Mechanics are around them, making sure that every system is in order. Overhead the sky is crisscrossed with searchlight beams woven into complicated patterns. They are signals for the returning RAF.

The crews are filing into the briefing room after a breakfast of black coffee, burned toast, and greasy eggs. Every man glances toward the target map as he enters, not really expecting to see anything. It is covered by black curtains; so is the board showing the formation assignments.

The benches fill up quickly. Commissioned officers — pilots, copilots, navigators, bombardiers — are mostly college men in their twenties. Gunners are youngest, eighteen and nineteen year-olds. The division or group commander may be in his late thirties and is the "Old Man."

A hush falls over the benches when the target map is uncovered. Then there are low groans and catcalls as they realize where they are being sent. Lengths of red wool are pinned to the map to mark the course. They stretch from the airfield deep into Germany.

Then someone pulls the string to open the blackboard curtains. More groans, mingled with sighs of relief. Some crews have drawn a high position in the high squadron, a safe place to be, usually. Another has drawn "Purple Heart Corner" or "Coffin Corner," the last plane in the lowest row of the formation.

"Tenn-hut!" someone calls, and the group snaps to attention as the officers enter the room. "At ease, gentlemen," says the CO and the briefing begins.

The CO starts by explaining the plan and why this mission is important. Then each specialist — S-2, weather, flak, flying control — goes over it from his own angle.

From the distance, from behind the mess hall and office buildings, comes a loud noise: the preflight warmup of B-17 engines early on a chilly morning. Farmers and villagers hear them too, as the sound comes rolling across the muddy fields. By 0530 very few people within miles of a bomber base are asleep.

The briefing ends with a time-tick, as watches are synchronized. The main group breaks into smaller groups. Navigators go into a nearby office to trace the routes on their maps. Bombardiers study target pictures with the group bombardier. The radiomen pick up the flimsies giving the day's call signals. They are called "flimsies" because they are made of rice-paper and can be eaten quickly in case there is danger of being captured. If the enemy found out the call signals, their radiomen could send our planes away from the target or lure them into a trap.

The combat crews are beginning to move into the equipment huts to collect their flying clothes. In the days before heated, pressurized cabins, cold was an airman's deadly enemy. Even in summer it is cold above the North Sea, where the temperature can drop to sixty below zero at twenty-five thousand feet. Frost smudges the plane's windshield and plexiglass bubbles, forcing the pilot to open the cockpit windows to equalize the temperatures. Wind whistles through the plane. Things were so bad that frostbite sent more Eighth fliers to the hospital in 1942 than enemy gunfire.

A flyer dresses like a North Pole explorer. His flight gear is bulky and heavy; its weight would drag him down like a stone if he fell into the ocean. Next to the skin he wears woolen underwear; it is hard and prickly, like steel wool. Then comes the sky-blue electrically heated "zoot suit." Over this goes a pair of fleece-lined leather pants and a sheepskin "bomber jacket." Flying gloves that reach to the elbow, sheepskin-lined boots, and "Mae West" life jacket complete the outfit for a while. Before combat an airman will put on a flak suit, body armor to protect his chest and back from shrapnel splinters. And if he's smart he'll take along a GI "tin pot" helmet for good measure.

Once dressed, the sooner into the air the better. No matter how cold it is on the ground, the airmen sweat. Beads of moisture run down foreheads, necks and underarms. The itching is awful. Everyone stinks like sweat-socks left in a locker too long.

Jeeps carry crewmembers to the waiting bombers. They look like whales patiently holding still to be groomed by swarms of lesser beings.

The ground crew is busy with last-minute instrument checks. Armorers and turret men make their rounds, asking if everything is okay. The gas truck is still topping the plane's four wing tanks. Every ounce of fuel is precious on a long flight.

The oxygen truck pulls away from the plane after checking the oxygen supply. A bomber's oxygen supply is stored in steel tanks and piped into the cockpit and other sections of the aircraft. When a flier has to move around, he disconnects from the supply line, hooks a walk-around bottle into his belt, and plugs the tubing of his oxygen mask into it. If he parachutes from over ten thousand feet he needs a bail-out bottle otherwise he'll suffocate in the thin air. (It takes about twenty minutes to parachute to earth from 35,000 feet.)

It is the pilot's right to name his airplane and no one else's. Some favor puns like *Wabbit Twacks* and *E-rat-icator*. Others like fierce names: *Hell's Angels, Butcher Shop, Alabama Exterminator, Whambam*. Women's names are also popular: *Peggy D, Rose O'Day, Betty Boop*. Finally there are always the few who make fun of everything: *Blood, Guts, and Rust, Lady Halitosis, Malfunction, All's Shot to Hell*.

Alongside each name is a painting, the airman's version of the figureheads carved on the old sailing ships. The painting might show a battle scene, a cartoon character,

Some British and American Bombs
of World War II

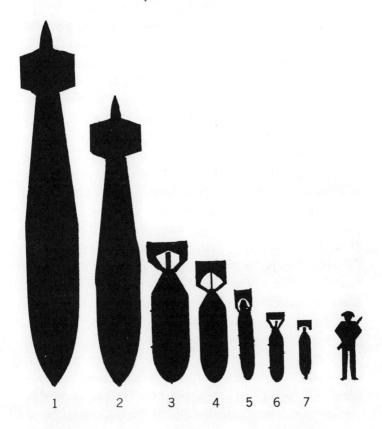

1. RAF 22,000-pound Grand Slam, the largest high-explosive bomb ever made
2. RAF 12,00-pound Tallboy, used for breaking through the concrete roofs of U-boat pens
3. USAAF 4000-pound Blockbuster
4. USAAF 2000-pound Blockbuster
5. USAAF 1000-pound armor-piercing bomb
6. USAAF 500-pound standard demolition bomb
7. USAAF 100-pound bomb with nose fuse; shell could also be filled with white phosporous to make the "Kenney Cocktail"

or a pinup girl. Beneath the pilot's window is a row of stenciled bombs and swastikas, one for each bombing mission or Nazi fighter downed by the ship's gunners.

A plane is said to be "operational" the moment the bombardier comes aboard. Everything the plane does is really to put him over the target with his bombsight and a load of bombs.

He is in charge of the Norden bombsight, one of the USAAF'S most closely guarded secrets. It is so secret that when not in use it is kept in a vault in a locked building patrolled by armed guards. When the bombardier carries it to the plane in its locked canvas case, he wears a pistol and will shoot anyone who tries to take it away from him. If his ship is crippled over enemy territory, he must destroy it in a special way no matter what that means for his personal safety.

Placing the bombsight on its stand in the plane's nose is only one of the bombardier's preflight tasks. He also looks after the bombs.

The Allies had different kinds of bombs for different purposes. *Armor-piercing* bombs had thick skins and sharp steel points that allowed them to break through a ship's hull or a tank's body and explode inside. *Anti-personnel* or *fragmentation* bombs had thin skins that exploded into hundreds of steel splinters when dropped on troops. *Incendiary* or fire bombs were loaded with chemicals that burned at high temperatures and usually weighed less than a hundred pounds apiece. *Demolition* bombs were the commonest; they were packed with a high explosive such as TNT or Amatol and were used to blow up bridges, buildings, and most other things.

Bombs came in all sizes, although the USAAF favored four sizes: 100, 250, 500 and 1000 pounds. The four thousand-pound "blockbuster" was seldom used, because the B-17 bomb rack had to be adjusted in order to be able to carry it. No USAAF plane could carry the RAF's monster bombs. Its Tallboy weighed twelve thousand pounds, but even that was a lightweight compared to the twenty-two thousand-pound Grand Slam, the blockbuster of blockbusters.

When the bomb handlers had parked their trailers under the B-17, they could not load each plane's bombs right away. Each bomb had first to be washed by hand like a tiny baby. Every piece of caked mud and dirt was scrubbed off the steel case until it shone, otherwise it wouldn't fall where the bombardier aimed. It would wobble in the wind, be thrown off course, and maybe ten men and an airplane would crash for nothing.

Once the bombs were clean, their tail fins were screwed into place. These, too, kept the bomb from wobbling and its nose pointed downward. When a bomb was first dropped, it fell lengthwise. After it had fallen a distance from the plane, the fins helped turn it so that it traveled the rest of the way point first.

The bomb handlers attach hooks to rings built into each bomb and carefully hoist them into the plane's belly. Even if one should break loose and fall, it wouldn't explode. It might smash a man's foot, but there was no chance of its going off.

Until they are "armed," bombs are nothing but masses of chemicals packed into steel containers. They look dangerous but are really harmless. You can jump on them, fling them onto concrete runways from speeding trucks, and hit them with hammers. They will just lie there.

Arming a bomb means screwing a fuse either into its nose or tail, tightening it with a wrench, and setting the safety catch. When the bomb begins to fall point downward, the rushing wind opens the safety catch, freeing a small propeller in the bomb's tip or tail. As the wind twirls the propeller, it unscrews the device that frees the firing pin inside the bomb and sets it to explode the instant it lands.

Before the plane can take off the bombardier must climb out onto the steel catwalk that divides the bomb bay. He inspects each bomb, giving the fuses a final twist with his hand to make sure they are tight. Then he signals the pilot to close the bomb bay doors.

0630. The planes are beginning to move. Flying Fortresses lumber toward the perimeter taxiway and then to the runway. There are nothing but airplanes, one behind the other.

A B-17 does not become airborne easily. She claws at the air, struggling to free her thirty-five tons of plane, bombs, and men from the ground. Once aloft, the motors strain, pulling her up at 300 feet a minute. This is the time when weaknesses appear and the most fuel is used up. From now until we sight the enemy coast there will be "aborts" (abortions) as planes develop troubles and turn back.

The next hour is the most dangerous time until the Luftwaffe rises to meet us. There are those planes that simply cannot rise from the ground. A tire blows, or a wheel collapses, throwing the plane over on its side in a ball of flame as its wing tanks explode and the bombs go off. Or it's a perfect liftoff and something goes wrong: we'll never know what, because the pieces are too small to put together. Some lift off, then fall into a nearby village. The worst accident happened at a small town, Freckleton, when a fully loaded bomber crashed into a schoolhouse.

Fog is an enemy also. There are sure to be accidents when taking off up through fog into a sky crowded with planes. Two columns of black smoke rise straight up

An armorer checks a two-thousand-pounder as it is about to be hoisted into the bomb bay of a Flying Fortress. These monsters were as harmless as tubes of concrete, until the fuses were inserted in their noses.

The combat box stagger

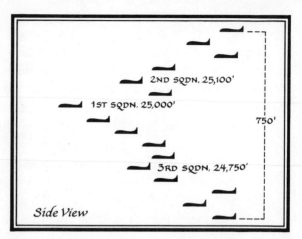

2ND SQDN. 25,100'

1ST SQDN. 25,000'

750'

3RD SQDN. 24,750'

Side View

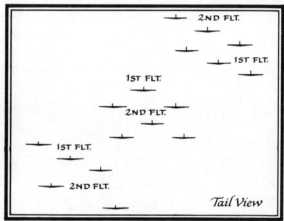

2ND FLT.

1ST FLT.

1ST FLT.

2ND FLT.

1ST FLT.

2ND FLT.

Tail View

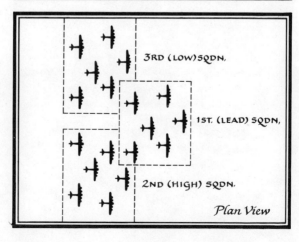

3RD (LOW) SQDN.

1ST. (LEAD) SQDN.

2ND (HIGH) SQDN.

Plan View

through the clouds, where a moment earlier there had been two planes, twenty men. Then a flash, a shock wave, and a wing fluttering to earth like a dry leaf.

0700. The formation is taking shape as each plane reaches assembly altitude. An "Assembly Ship" painted with all the colors of a clown's costume is there waiting to position the plane. This one is called *"Little Cookie,"* because it is covered with yellow polka dots. Using radio voice messages and colored flares, the controller assembles each group and heads it toward the meeting point.

The sight from the ground is breathtaking. The sky for miles around is filled with tiny silvery slivers of light, each trailing a long white tail of condensed vapor, the "contrail."

The earth trembles. Farmhouse windows rattle. Tiles shake loose from church rooftops as the air fleet thunders overhead.

As they near the meeting point, converging groups, dozens of planes by now, are orbiting in wide circles around a radio compass beacon called "Splasher." The whole force will be put together here before heading for Germany.

The force will be assembled into a formation known as the "combat box stagger." This is a technical USAAF term, although the idea behind it is simple. There is safety in numbers, in the massed firepower of tightly packed formations of heavy bombers. And the tighter the better.

As the separate groups home in on the Splasher they are divided into three squadrons of six planes each, eighteen planes in all. These squadrons are formed into horizontal Vs and stacked slightly above and to the side of one another. The combat "box" is complete and extends 750 feet from top to bottom.

The first box is then joined by two others to form a combat wing, "staggered" so that there is a lead box, a low box down to the left, and a high box up to the right. The whole wing of three boxes, nine Vs, fifty-four planes, forms a flying wedge that stretches three thousand feet from top to bottom.

This system allows for uncovering every gun in the formation. No matter how skilled the enemy fighter pilot, there is no way to come near a combat wing without running into a crisscrossing fire from at least 200 heavy machine guns. No wonder no USAAF bomber force ever turned back once it had been committed to battle.

Every bomber protects every other bomber in the interlocking formation. But let a plane drop out of formation and it doesn't have a chance. The enemy fighters will catch up with it and drop it quickly.

The planes are still climbing and at ten thousand feet the pilot reminds the crew over the interphone to put on oxygen masks. The pure oxygen flows in with a hiss the moment the valve is turned.

There are whitecaps far below, glistening as the salt spray catches the sun's rays. Toward the horizon to the northeast looms the low hump of the Dutch coast. Suddenly, from nowhere, the sky above, below, behind, is filled with quickly moving shapes: fighters.

The yellow, blue, white, and red "targets" on their wings and fuselage signal they're friendly. They are "Spits" — Spitfires — 250 of them, the fighter escort. They bank slightly to let the bomber crews see their insignia; there's no point taking chances with trigger-happy gunners.

Pretend that a Flying Fortress is a motorboat and that its propellers are slicing through water instead of air. The boatman is lucky; he can dodge rough water if he sees it in time. Not a bomber pilot. As the air divisions, combat wings, and combat boxes come barreling through the sky one after another, they add to the air's normal restlessness. If they were visible the slipstreams, spun backward by their propellers, each fifty times larger than an outbord motor's, would look like tornado funnels. And they hit just as hard.

Each formation whips up the air, lashing the one behind it. Rivets snap. Strained fuselage seams split open. Thirty-five tons of airplane bounces like a balloon in the wind.

The pilot must ride this whirlwind every second all the way. His hands turn white as he grips the controls. His muscles ache and he loses feeling in his fingers. Beads of sweat dangle from his nose and chin, forming a salty little pool at the bottom of the oxygen mask. But he hangs on, knowing that a false move will send the ship crashing into a neighbor in the tightly packed formation. By the time he lands again, the pilot will have sweated off several pounds.

The target is inside Germany, about 550 miles from the coast. At the 325-mile point the Spits wag their wings as a goodluck signal and peel off for home. They are running low on fuel and can't take the bombers any further without harming themselves. Bomber crews blow kisses as the Spits turn away, leaving them alone in the big sky.

"Big friends, little friends." The contrails of a group of American fighters are all that is visible as they prowl ahead, keeping a sharp lookout for Luftwaffe "bandits."

German radar locked onto the formation even as it was climbing over the English Channel. There may even

be a B-17 in a rear box plotting the course and radioing it back to Luftwaffe fighter control.

Whenever a B-17 came down pretty much intact in occupied Europe, German mechanics tried to make it flyable. If they succeeded, the plane was sent with its original markings to join Eighth bomber formations. Being tracked this way had become such a problem that strays were not allowed to join the boxes and were shot at if they didn't take no for an answer.

Reports of location, altitude, and course are pouring into the "Battle Opera Houses," or central command stations of Luftwaffe fighter divisions. These are giant underground bunkers built along the aerial highways of Europe and are strange places. The air in them is heavy with the smell of unwashed bodies and stale cigarette smoke. The only sound is the humming of ventilators, the clacking of teletypes, and the murmur of dozens of telephone operators wearing earphones and mouthpieces.

The center of attraction is a large panel of frosted glass, a map-screen upon which dots of light and illuminated writing are projected. This writing has all the information one needs to find and shoot down invading aircraft. The fighter controllers are seated in front of the map-screen. Each *Jagdfuehrer* is in touch with a fighter base by telephone. He can receive, interpret, and send information to fighters inside of a minute. The English meaning of *Jadgfuehrer* is "leader of the hunt," and that is exactly what he is.

ACHTUNG! ACHTUNG! FEINDLICHE FLUG-ZEUGE! "Attention! Attention! Enemy aircraft!"

At these words alarm bells ring in the day rooms of dozens of fighter squadrons along the route.

As the bombers fly onward, the pattern of the coming battle is being set by men not seen. ME-109s and FW-190s are already taking off singly or in pairs. They sweep around over their fields, coming in low to gain speed for the climb to altitude. There are also sleek Junkers JU-88 twin-engined bombers rigged as gunships. And twin-engined Messerschmitt ME-110 fighter-bombers carrying *Schraege Musik* (jazz music), a pair of upward-pointing cannon mounted behind the pilot's cockpit. All he has to do is slide beneath a bomber and fire a short burst to tear open its belly and set off its bombs.

The bombers are ready for them. Everybody except the pilot and copilot is manning a gun. Only these two are seated during battle, each strapped into his seat at the controls with belts and shoulder harness. If they are blown away from the controls it's "curtains" for the rest of the crew.

The gunners fight in unnatural, cramped positions. Bombardier and navigator crouch in the ship's nose with a machine gun apiece. They and the radioman who stands at his gun position are the only gunners who are not experts; the others have spent months learning to use their weapons. The two waist gunners are standing on either side of the ship with a machine gun each. Their windows are wide open and the rushing air slashes their faces like icicle knives. The top turret man, who is also flight engineer, stands with his twin machine guns. The tail gunner kneels in front of his two machine guns as if in mock prayer. The ball turret gunner's position is the most uncomfortable; he must painfully twist his body into a half-ball to meet the curve of the turret. Isolated as he is underneath the plane, he is least likely to be able to bail out or walk away from a crash.

The top and ball turrets are something special: rotating steel and plexiglass blisters powered by electric batteries. The gunner braces his hands against bars like

BATTLE STATIONS
Crew Positions in the Flying Fortress and the Liberator

bicycle handle bars. Pressure to the right or left turns the whole turret in that direction, slowly or quickly, depending on the amount of pressure. Downward pressure raises the guns, upward pressure lowers them. Both guns are fired together by a trigger located under the gunner's right finger. The gunsight is in the middle cross hairs of a standing glass; the gunner sights with his left eye.

The Browning .50-caliber machine gun, or "big fifty," is the weapon of choice on USAAF bombers. It *is* big. A machine gun's caliber, or size, is the width of the inside of the barrel measured in fractions of an inch. Thus a .50-caliber gun has a half-inch wide barrel and fires half-inch wide bullets. This gun weighs sixty-five pounds and can fire 575 slugs a minute at a speed of twenty-nine hundred feet a second. These slugs can go through an inch of steel armor plate, turning a fighter into a smoking pile of junk in seconds. Some Eighth gunners are so fond of their weapons that the night before a mission they clean every part with soap and water and take them to bed to prevent rust.

Every fifth slug in the belt is a tracer filled with a kind of fireworks that ignites as it speeds through the air, leaving a long straight line of light. Tracers help a gunner see how he's shooting and correct his aim if necessary.

The ship's interphones come alive. The tail and ball turret gunners have spotted "bandits" at the same time. They come up from behind and fly alongside a bomber, looking it over from a safe distance. Then they whiz ahead, climbing as if the bomber were standing still.

There are ME-109s painted coal-black except for their yellow noses. The FW-190s are completely yellow and polished to a high shine. Other planes are silver or have black bellies and cream upper surfaces, or white bellies and striped tops of different colors.

Besides being attractive, these colors and patterns are useful in battle. Unusual markings lessen the chance of friendly planes firing on one another. Brightly colored upper surfaces and dull bellies have another advantage: like a butterfly's wings on a sunny day, the colorful upper sides dazzle the hunter and then "disappear" when the insect suddenly banks, revealing their dull undersides. Sometimes the undersides of the Flying Fortresses were painted light blue, which helped them blend into the sky when seen from below.

Between the enemies there is the respect that comes from fear. The Luftwaffe pilot of 1943 was a tough customer. The Knight's Cross worn at his throat had been earned in battle against the Allies. No one who flew in bombers made fun of him.

The Germans had their problems too. They had never seen anything like the U.S. bomber formations before. Their old, battle-tested tactics were useless against them. Attacking from the rear means closing at slow speed against massed fire from a group's tail guns. Attacking from above or below, singly or in pairs, can't bring enough firepower to bear to knock a bomber down at the first pass. German fighter pilots learned the hard way that they needed at least twenty-five hits with .20-mm shells to destroy a Flying Fortress. (There are about 25 millimeters to an inch, meaning that a .20-mm cannon fires a shell that is almost an inch wide.)

The Luftwaffe's 600 day fighters were commanded by Adolf Galland, who in 1941, at the age of 29, became

There were no "aborts" over Germany. Although the wing of this Flying Fortress is burning, it must continue in formation to the target. Enemy fighters will destroy it if it tries to return to base alone.

Hitler's youngest general. Galland formed the Rosarius Traveling Circus to train fighter pilots. The Circus was made up of captured but flyable American aircraft. It visited Luftwaffe fighter squadrons to allow the pilots to become familiar with their flying qualities by flying them themselves.

Galland also asked for suggestions for dealing with the Americans from combat units, the aviation industry, and the German people. When suggestions poured in by the hundreds, he created the Twenty-fifth Experimental Commando to test the best ones under actual battle conditions.

The American bombers are the guinea pigs this morning. Some of the beautiful fighters that have just flown by climb above the group and drop their own bombs; they're bombing the bombers. Others drop aerial mines that drift into the B-17's paths on parachutes. FW-190s trail long cables with electrically detonated bombs dangling on the end.

German fighters were armed with some nasty missile weapons. As well as their normal machine guns and cannon they also carried large cannon. The two-engined Messerschmitt ME-410 "destroyer" carried an armored-car cannon weighing a ton. This monster stuck out nine feet in front of the plane and, as the crews said, if its shells missed a bomber the gun itself could always be used as a battering ram.

Air-to-air rockets are the scariest and most dangerous of fighter weapons. Their white smoke trails head toward a plane, but the formations are so tightly packed that it can't move out of the way without crashing into another ship. A rocket can easily tear a wing off a B-17 or carry away a whole cockpit, men and all. Sometimes a fighter pilot gets lucky: one fellow hit a B-17 which then crashed into two others, for a loss of three planes, thirty men, from a single shot.

The best fighter tactic was worked out by one of Galland's officers, Oberleutnant Egon Meyer. Meyer discovered that fighters scored well if they attacked head-on in groups of four abreast, one group following another. True, they also met the B-17 combat boxes' firepower head-on, but at a closing speed of over 600 miles an hour (the fighters' plus the bombers' combined speeds) they could strike and zip away in a few seconds.

That's today's program. After some false moves to locate the "green" gunners who'll fire before they're in range, they charge.

The orange-yellow lights flash along the outer edges of the fighters' wings. As they come nearer they start a half-roll, keeping their fire on a single target all the while. We can see the pilots' heads as they speed by, maybe ten feet from our right wing.

The interphones of fifty-four Flying Fortresses crackle with excited calls. The story of an air battle is told not in complete sentences but in clipped phrases, each with a story behind it. One-oh-nines at ten o'clock. . . . Hold on. . . . Steady. . . . Steady. . . . Lead him, for Christ's sake, lead him. . . . Shorter bursts, man, you're wasting ammo . . . Roger . . . Look out, ball turret . . . One-nine-oh. . . . Got him, got him. . . . Hot damn!"

Nothing shows war's chanciness better than an air battle. Life and death are measured in hundredths of an inch. A rocket blows out a man-sized hunk of fuselage near the top turret and a fourteen-inch piece of steel tears the seat off the gunner's pants without scratching his backside. A waist gunner slips on the shell casings that litter the floor just as a steel splinter nicks his ear lobe. A miss is as good as a mile, but it will give you the jitters for weeks afterward.

Tondelayo in the 379th Group takes a .20-mm shell in a gas tank and nothing happens. Nothing happens! The ship *should* have blown up instantly.

Later, when the pilot asks the ground crew chief for the shell as a souvenir, he asks *which* shell, for he found eleven unexploded cannon shells in the ship's gas tanks. The shells are opened and found to be without explosive charges. Onc shell contains a tightly rolled piece of paper with a message in the Czechoslovakian language. Translation: "This is all we can do for you now." That's enough. Chalk up another victory to those silent soldiers of the underground in Nazi-occupied Europe.

An aerial battle is a swirling, formless confusion. So much is happening at once, but everything happens quickly and is over soon. A bomber gracefully slides out of formation with its left inboard motor burning and explodes with a WHUFF. The sky becomes a junkyard as far as the eye can see. All sorts of wreckage falls heavily to earth in a straight line or flutters down lazily. An Eighth bombardier described it:

> Swinging their yellow noses around in a wide U-turn, a twelve-ship squadron of ME-109s came in from twelve to two o'clock in pairs and in fours, and the main event was on.
>
> A shining silver object sailed over our right wing. I recognized it as a main exit door. Seconds later, a dark object came hurtling through the formation, barely missing several props. It was a man, clasping his knees to his head, revolving like a diver

in a triple somersault. I didn't see his chute open.

A B-17 turned gradually out of the formation to the right, maintaining altitude. In a split second, the B-17 completely disappeared in a brilliant explosion, from which the only remains were four small balls of fire, the fuel tanks, which were quickly consumed as they fell earthward.

Our airplane was endangered by falling debris. Emergency hatches, exit doors, prematurely opened parachutes, bodies, and assorted fragments of B-17s and Hun fighters breezed past us in the slip stream.

I watched two fighters explode not far beneath, disappearing in sheets of orange flame, B-17s dropping out in every state of distress, from engines on fire to control surfaces shot away, friendly and enemy parachutes floating down, and, on the green carpet far behind us, numerous funeral pyres of smoke from fallen fighters, marking our trail. The sight was fantastic; it surpassed fiction.

On we flew through the strewn wake of a desperate air battle, where disintegrating aircraft were commonplace and sixty chutes in the air at one time were hardly worth a second look.

I watched a B-17 turn slowly out to the right with its cockpit a mass of flames. The copilot crawled out of his window, held on with one hand, reached back for his chute, buckled it on, let go, and was whisked back into the horizontal stabilizer. I believe the impact killed him. His chute didn't open.

(Quoted in *Target: Germany*, Simon & Schuster, New York, 1943.)

"Flak so thick you can walk on it." This photo, taken from the cockpit of a nearby plane, shows a Flying Fortress plowing through heavy flak over Germany. In spite of the explosions surrounding it, the plane's bomb bay doors are open and it is making a run on its target.

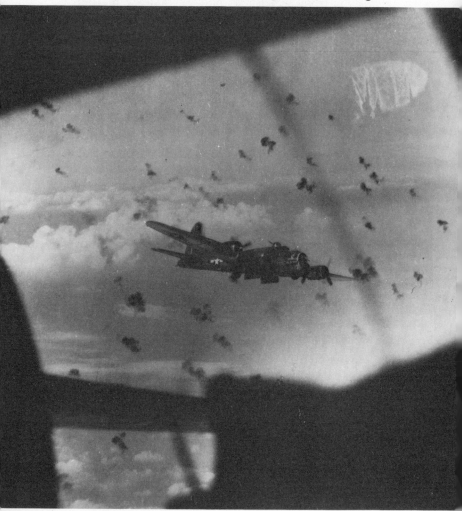

The sky becomes filled with parachutes. Sometimes an FW-190 streaks by a helpless man and the pilot squeezes off a short burst, leaving him dangling limp in his parachute harness. A wise man falls through the battle area, not pulling the ripcord until he is about fifteen hundred feet from the ground and out of the fighters' reach.

Suddenly the fighters are gone. They've disappeared as if by magic. This doesn't mean that Jerry's given up. The bombers are nearing a likely target and the fighters have moved aside to give the flak a clear field of fire.

"Flak" is a shortening of *(Fl)ieger(a)bwehr(k)anone,* German for "antiaircraft gun." The Americans and the British have taken over the word because it is short and snappy, like a flak burst.

There were two types of flak over Germany. Light flak was mainly .37-mm cannon that were dangerous up to ten thousand feet. Heavy flak was .88-mm cannon that could hurl a shell three inches in diameter as high as forty thousand feet.

Some flak shells had clock mechanisms timed to explode at a certain altitude into wing-tearing, fuselage-ripping fragments. Others had fuses so sensitive that the slightest touch of a wing, or even a raindrop, would set them off. Antiaircraft shells were so powerful that any plane within fifty feet of an explosion was sure to be hit by high-speed steel fragments.

The Germans knew that it was almost as hard to shoot down any one plane in a formation as it was to bag any one bird in a large flock. The trick was not to aim at individuals but to pour as many shells as possible into a fixed part of the sky. In the "flak trap" and "box bar-

Bombs away. The Flying Fortresses in this "box" have either just released their sticks of bombs or are preparing to release them.

rage" hundreds of guns fired from every angle into a certain area along the bombers' target approach. If they destroyed the lead plane in a combat wing so much the better, because this confused the other bombardiers who release their loads on the lead bombardier's signal. Even

so, it cost Jerry 8,243 light and heavy flak shells to shoot down one four-engined bomber.

The navigator is on the interphone: "We're at the IP," the Initial Point where we turn right and begin our run on the target. There is about fifteen minutes to go from here, and the pilot calls for a head count. The crew sounds off in order, beginning from the tail: "Number one check. Number two check. Number three check. . . ."

The Germans are doing their best to hide the target.

Smoke screen units are puffing huge white clouds that rise slowly and blanket the area. Piles of wood gathered at key points are set on fire to fool the bombers into dropping the bombs too early. Whale-sized barrage balloons, hydrogen-filled sacks attached to wire rope cables, float above the target area. Barrage balloons can spoil a bombardier's aim, while the cables can slice a plane's wing off.

The planes reach the AP, the Aiming Point where the bombs are released. There is a WOOMPF, followed by PING, PING, PING. A flak shell has exploded, sending steel splinters against the side of a ship.

The copilot calls: "Bomb bay doors in the lead ship are opening." The bomb bay doors on the other Flying Fortresses are opening, too. The bomb run, lasting usually six minutes, is on.

The ship below on the left catches fire forward of the bomb bay and disappears in a flash and a shower of red-hot sparks.

And still the bombers fly on, nearer, always nearer to the drop point. Another ship catches fire. It is trailing a sheet of orange flame that stretches from its left outboard motor to the tail, but continues the run. There's nothing else it can do, for even if it could drop out of formation the Focke-Wulfs prowling nearby would be on it in seconds. There are no aborts over Germany.

The bombardier is flying the ship with his automatic control equipment linked to the Norden bombsight. A long "stick," or row, of bombs begins to fall from the lead ship and instantly every plane in the combat wing is dropping its load.

Everyone feels both terror and relief. Bombs from

American troops examine the wreckage caused by Allied bombers in a German railway yard they have captured.

the upper ships in the box fall past planes lower in the formation. They whistle as they go by. And they are within arms length of the window. Sometimes they hit friendly aircraft, which either explode or are so badly damaged that they go into a spin, falling into the city below.

The moment the bombs are gone, the ship, suddenly free of their weight, lurches upward. A feeling of relief runs through the ship even before the bombardier cries "Bombs away!"

The pilot strikes the control column with his fist for good luck. The copilot raps the instrument panel for the same reason. Up until now they've been flying 100 percent for Uncle Sam, but from here on in they fly for themselves. There are loud explosions far below one after another, then clouds of thick dirty smoke.

The flight home is a carbon copy of the flight over. Flak is taking its toll. Planes damaged on the way to the target are showing their wounds. They lose speed and are unable to tuck themselves into the formation for safety. Gradually a bomber flying on two engines, or trailing smoke, or with damaged control cables, falls behind. There's nothing to be done for him as the Focke-Wulfs move in.

Everyone is tired and looks it. Hours of heavy work at high altitude have left their mark, especially on the gunners. Gunsmoke has turned their faces black. They have been sweating freely in spite of the bitter cold, and icicles hang from their hair and eyelashes.

As the bombers reach the brown and green lacework of Holland hundreds of fast-moving specks twinkle in the distance. They are Eighth fighters sent to bring the planes the rest of the way home. There's some annoying flak from the Dutch offshore islands but no more enemy fighters.

The English coast appears as the planes begin to lose altitude. By now they are below oxygen altitude; it is good to tear off the clammy masks. Only twenty minutes to go before landing.

1130 hours. The bombers have been airborne for five hours and are expected home any minute. At airfields throughout East Anglia, the ground crews silently gather in bunches along the hangar line. Officers crowd the balconies of control towers. Ambulances and fire trucks stand by with purring engines. Firemen looking like aliens from outer space perspire patiently in their asbestos suits and helmets.

Soon the air fleet is thundering overhead. Farmers stop behind the plow, children forget their schoolyard games. Everyone is looking skyward and counting. How many are missing today?

The combat wings separate into groups, each heading for its own field. They circle waiting for Flying Control to "talk" them down, to give them landing instructions. Red flares arch from the top hatches of some aircraft, a signal that wounded or dead are aboard. These ships always get clearance to land first.

As each plane with casualties touches down, bouncing and screeching along the runway, an ambulance races after it at top speed, pulling up alongside just as it stops. Time means life. Some airfields are far from major hospitals, and rather than shake up the wounded for an hour on bumpy country roads, bombers no longer fit for combat are used as hospital planes. The dead travel more slowly, to the American military cemetary at Cambridge.

"Coming Home on a Wing and a Prayer," a popular 1943 song, tells what it's like after the planes have landed. Again and again planes have been given up for lost, only to return. Every outfit has its stories of B-17 ruggedness. A bomber's main wing spar is cut by flak; seven hours later, after battling fighters and diving through a hole in the clouds, it brings its crew home with only the thin metal skin holding the wing together.

Or a ME-109 attacks one of the Ninety-seventh Bomb Group. The Nazi pilot is killed by the ship's gunners and his plane tumbles wildly out of control. But instead of heading earthward, it hits the B-17 at a closing speed of 500 miles an hour, nearly cutting the fuselage in half and carrying away half the tail. Still the pilot completes the mission and lands safely ninety minutes later.

Bringing home a seriously damaged bomber is dangerous. The engines may conk out before touchdown, or oil pressure may go to zero, sending the unlubricated propellers racing out of control until they melt, hurling gobs of red-hot steel into the cockpit. Bailing out over England is as dangerous as bailing out anywhere else. Parachutists can break their necks. They can drown in lakes, pulled down by their water soaked chutes. They can be electrocuted on power lines. Yet most come down safely; in fact, some have a lot of fun. A gunner from the 309th Bomb Group was knocked cold on hitting the ground. Waking up, he found himself in the arms of a pretty English girl who was kissing him. He thought he had died and gone to heaven.

One of the most famous photographs of World War II.
This B-17 returned to base after nearly being sliced in
half by a ME-109 that spun out of control when its pilot
was killed and crashed into the bomber's rear section.

The ground crews are waiting as the planes come to
a stop. These are the first people the bomber group sees
after a mission and it is they who learn about it first. But
even as they talk, the mechanics are swarming over the
ship like fussy housekeepers. One measures flak holes for
metal patches. Another checks that new supercharger
part, or sweeps up empty shell casings. By nightfall she'll
be ready to fly again.

As for her crew, there's still the debriefing. The combat crews are gathering in the briefing room, where intelligence officers are waiting for their "hot news." Hot coffee and doughnuts will help calm them down and pull their thoughts together.

Each crew is around a separate table with everyone answering questions at once. "Where did you meet the first flak?" "How did that FW-190 come in?" "Any ideas about how we can do better next time?"

Debriefing is over quickly and they troop out, some heading for the barracks, other for the mess hall. Hot food, hot showers, sleep: these are all they want.

Miles away at Eighth Bomber Command headquarters the lights are burning late. Soon the teletypes will be clattering louder than ever.

4

Learning the Hard Way

USAAF bombers visited hundreds of enemy targets in Europe in the nearly two-and-a-half years after the Casablanca Conference. Each target was like a tiny piece of a giant jigsaw puzzle—Germany's power to make war. Each target had to be blown up or burned out before Hitler's Third Reich could be brought to its knees. Yet every target was not equally important, or each mission equally memorable. A few missions will be remembered as long as people make war above the clouds.

One of these missions had to do with oil, the only piece of the jigsaw puzzle that fit in with all the others. For without oil and the gasoline made from it, no part of Hitler's war machine could move.

One-third of Hitler's oil came from a single town, Ploesti, in Rumania. This unattractive town is located near Bucharest, Rumania's capital, in the southern part of the country. It sits on a plain at the center of a spider's web of oil derricks, pipelines, refineries, cooling towers, and gasoline storage tank farms. What better place for USAAF bombers to light fires? A few dozen bombs in the right places and Ploesti would go up like a barrel of fireworks.

On the morning of August 1, 1943, five groups of Eighth and Ninth Air Force Liberators — 178 planes — lifted off the airstrip at Bengazi, Libya, in North Africa. The plan of Operation TIDAL WAVE was to head northward across the Mediterranean Sea, keeping low to stay under enemy radar. When the planes reached the target, they would attack at treetop level, drop their bombs, and escape before the enemy knew what hit him.

There is an old army word that describes what happened once the Ploesti mission got started. The word is "snafu," a shortening of "(s)ituation (n)ormal, (a)ll (f)ouled (u)p." TIDAL WAVE was the snafu of snafus. First, ten of the B-24s turned back to Bengazi with engine and other troubles. Then *Wingo Wango* suddenly nosed down at full speed and exploded in the sea, taking with it the mission's chief navigator.

No one could know how great his loss would be until the planes neared the Initial Point for the final turn to the target. The navigator of the lead group turned too soon, drawing the next group after him. The following three groups, noticing the error, stayed on course.

But it was already too late. Within minutes the first two groups saw a strange city rising up ahead of them: Bucharest! Realizing their error, they turned sharply to the left and headed for Ploesti.

Bearing down on Ploesti. A group of Liberators fly through
clouds of smoke rising from oil-storage tank farms that
have just been bombed by another group.

Now everything began to fall apart. Air raid spotters in Bucharest sounded the alarm and in seconds the roofs of houses began to roll back, uncovering batteries of those terrible .88s. The sides of railroad boxcars fell away and haystacks opened up to sprout machine guns. Worst of all, yellow-nosed fighters were streaking down every runway in the area.

The battlefield that day was a narrow avenue thirteen miles long and fifty feet high on the way into Ploesti. Machine gun bullets fell and rose in sheets as the Liberator and Luftwaffe gunners shot it out at point-blank range. Gun crews fired .88s like shotguns over open sights; sometimes they fired *downward* from hillsides at the oncoming bombers.

It was a wild scene over the oil refineries. Planes sped in from every direction. The two groups that had gone to Bucharest came up from the southeast instead of down from the northeast as planned. Unable to find their targets, they bombed whatever looked good. Meanwhile the other groups approaching from the right direction found their targets already bombed, or couldn't find them at all due to rising clouds of black smoke.

Planes flew through the smoke, only to meet a smokestack dead ahead. Or they had to dodge other planes coming at them from the opposite direction or cutting across their flight path.

Planes bearing down on a refinery were blown out of the air by time bombs dropped by an earlier group; the low-flying planes used time bombs to allow them to escape the blasts of their own weapons. Other planes flew through walls of flame and exploding gasoline storage tanks, coming through scorched and filled with smoke.

A B-24 Liberator, crippled by uncontrollable fires, is about to go into its death-plunge.

Pilots had the hair on their arms singed and their nostrils filled with the foul odor of burned hair.

A boilerhouse hit by a bomber seconds before exploded just as another plane passed overhead, swatting it down like a moth caught in a blowtorch. Long slashes of fire scarred the land as low-flying planes were hit by flak and skidded out of control at 250 miles an hour.

Forty-one Liberators went down over Ploesti or near it; another fourteen were lost for other reasons or forced down by battle damage or when they ran out of fuel. Five Congressional Medals of Honor were awarded for TIDAL WAVE, more than for any military action in history; 310 men died.

The Liberators left Ploesti a sea of flame. Yet it was not knocked out of the war. The oil field and its equipment had never been worked as hard as possible, so it was easy to cut damaged units out of the system and hook up others. The Nazis used gangs of slave laborers to repair the damage in a few months. It took another year of bombing, this time by B-17s and B-24s operating from newly captured bases in Italy, to put Ploesti out of the war.

Ball bearings are almost as important as oil in modern war. Nearly every machine and weapon of the Second World War had metal parts that gave off heat and wore out when they rubbed against one another. Ball bearings are tiny steel balls that are placed where the metal parts touch; they make the parts roll rather than rub against one another, preventing wear-out.

The Luftwaffe used large numbers of ball bearings in its planes. For example, a Junkers JU-88 medium bomber needed 1,056 of them for its body, plus hundreds of others for its engines and controls. Clearly, the Nazi war machine would grind to a halt if its ball bearing plants were destroyed. And what made these plants even more tempting was the fact that at least half of them were in the one town of Schweinfurt in the southern part of Germany.

Here was the problem. Schweinfurt, which means "pig-crossing," was deep inside German territory and well protected. The Eighth would have to fly along a pathway guarded by hundreds of .88s and fighters. It would have to go in in daylight without fighter escort, locate each factory building, and bomb it. The price would be high, everyone knew, but one worth paying in order to cripple the Luftwaffe.

Schweinfurt was attacked on August 17, 1943, with a loss of thirty-six Flying Fortresses. But the ball bearing factories were not destroyed. The Eighth returned on October 14, 1943, fighting one of the most terrible air battles in history. Even today the thought of "Second Schweinfurt," or "Black Thursday," sends shivers through American airmen.

The mission began with catcalls as the target maps were opened and the crews saw where they were being sent. The plan was simple: 291 Flying Fortresses would drop their fighter cover at the Belgian-German border, punch through to Schweinfurt by themselves, and wipe it off the map. As the crews filed out of the briefing rooms their commanders wished them "good luck, good shooting, and good bombing."

Everything went smoothly for the bombers until the American fighters had to turn for home. The last sight many of the fighter pilots had of their "big friends" was of bombers spinning to earth in flames. The Luftwaffe had been waiting just outside the American fighters' range and attacked with everything it had the moment they turned back.

A bomber pilot tells what happened that morning: "I feel McLaughlin's hand on my arm. It is a hard grip and I see he is looking down and ahead. I lean over, craning my neck, following his eyes. A few hundred feet ahead of us a bomber has been hit by a rocket. I catch sight of it just as the right wing starts to fold upward.

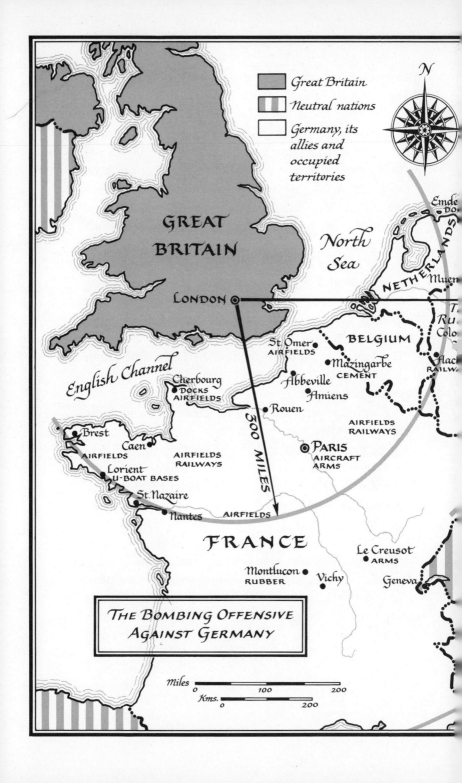

Great Britain
Neutral nations
Germany, its allies and occupied territories

N

GREAT BRITAIN

North Sea

NETHERLANDS

Emde

Muen

LONDON

St.Omer AIRFIELDS

BELGIUM

Ru

Colo

Mazingarbe CEMENT

Flac RAILWA

English Channel

Cherbourg DOCKS AIRFIELDS

Abbeville

Amiens

Brest

AIRFIELDS

Caen

AIRFIELDS RAILWAYS

Rouen

AIRFIELDS RAILWAYS

300 MILES

PARIS AIRCRAFT ARMS

Lorient U-BOAT BASES

St.Nazaire

Nantes

AIRFIELDS

FRANCE

Le Creusot ARMS

Montlucon RUBBER

Vichy

Geneva

THE BOMBING OFFENSIVE AGAINST GERMANY

Miles
0   100   200

Kms.
0   100   200

The fuselage opens like an eggshell, and a man dressed in a flying suit spins clear out in front. I see the pilot still at the controls, and then the plane is swept with flames. The right wing breaks free, and with the two engines still spinning it drifts to the rear, flaming at the ragged end. The shattered mess disappears under our right wing, and the sky is clean again. It happens instantly, but to me it is like a slow-motion movie scene."

Some crewmen, noticing dozens of huge red flashes as they turned on the Initial Point, shouted that the Germans were using red-colored flak shells, not realizing that what they saw was really bombers exploding in the combat wings up ahead. Men watched helplessly, tears rolling down their cheeks, as a tongue of flame leaped from a tear in a wing of a nearby plane, fed on the fuel, and turned the whole fuselage into a torch.

Schweinfurt was plastered with bombs but still not destroyed. The Germans feared that another attack would finish it off before they could scatter the ball bearing factories all over the country, but they needn't have worried. The Eighth was in no condition to return to Schweinfurt any time soon. Sixty B-17s, 600 men, had been lost in action; another five planes had to be abandoned over England, and seventeen were so badly damaged that they never flew again. Only fifty planes returned without holes in them made by enemy gunfire.

The survivors who stood around the debriefing tables were tired and sick at heart. A battle-hardened infantryman would have known at once that some of them were shell-shocked. No laughter, no flood of words this time. Men stood there, hands shaking, eyes watery, muttering answers to the intelligence officers' questions. Others broke down and cried openly.

"Any questions?" an officer asked.

"Yeah. Give us fighters for escort!"

Even before Second Schweinfurt the USAAF chiefs had begun to search for a fighter that could escort bombers to any target, fight, and escort them home. The best answer turned out to be the easiest: increase the range of the fighters they already had by fitting them with drop-tanks. These were extra gasoline tanks mounted under the fighter's belly that could be dropped when empty or before combat.

At the time of Second Schweinfurt, the Eighth de-

The Republic P-47 Thunderbolt was affectionately known as "the jug" because its body reminded pilots of a milk bottle with wings. It had eight .50-caliber machine guns, almost as many as carried by the bombers it was supposed to protect.

The P-51 Mustang spelled the Luftwaffe's doom. It could outfly and outshoot any propeller-driven plane the Germans had; it could even hold its own against the early jet fighters. Even today it is prized by air-racing enthusiasts.

pended on the Republic P-47 Thunderbolt, nicknamed "the Jug," because it looked like a milk bottle with wings. The P-47 was a fine plane, but also the heaviest propeller driven fighter ever built, weighing in at twenty-one thousand pounds. Its combat radius was only about 175 miles, or from the English coast to Paris and back. Larger and larger drop-tanks were added until early 1944, when the 150-gallon size gave it a combat radius of 425 miles. This was better than before, but still not good enough for bombing missions deep inside Germany.

The real turning point in the air war came only a few weeks after Second Schweinfurt, in November, 1943, when two new fighters began to arrive in England. The first of these, the Lockheed P-38 Lightning, was a high-flying, twin-engined fighter. Fast and tough, it was the first American plane to face the ME-109 on equal terms. When fitted with 108-gallon droptanks, the Lightning could range up to 585 miles from its bases. It deserved its German nickname of *die Gabelschwanz Teufel,* "the fork-tailed Devil."

But it was the North American P-51 Mustang that finally spelled the end for the Luftwaffe. What an airplane! It's six .50-caliber machine guns could take care of anything with wings, and it flew like a dream. It could do 487 miles an hour at twenty-five thousand feet and 427 miles an hour at forty-two thousand feet, its top altitude. Not even the FW-190 could stand up to the Mustang for long, especially after two 108-gallon wing drop-tanks increased its combat radius to 850 miles. The bomber crews soon grew to love their "little friends," the tiny "peashooters" that escorted them right down the Luftwaffe's throat and back.

The fighter pilot of the Second World War was a special person, more like the freewheeling knight of the Middle Ages than today's jet pilot. He was younger than the jet pilot, often in his early twenties. Youth was important. It meant quick reflexes at a time when humans

and not computers had to make split-second decisions meaning life or death. It also meant raw physical strength at a time when sky fighting demanded the stamina of a football player.

The cold at high altitudes was hard on a person, but the "G" force (gravity) was terrible. Power dives and sharp turns in unpressurized flight suits put terrific strain on heart, lungs, and blood vessels. Turns in which the pilot's feet traveled along the outer edge of the plane's curving path pulled blood away from the eyes and brain. At first the pilot would "gray-out," his vision becoming blurred and everything turning gray; a few seconds later he "blacked out" altogether. But turns in which the pilot's head pointed outward, such as the outside loop, had the opposite effect. The eyes and brain became flooded with blood. The pilot then suffered "redout," as everything turned red and he developed a splitting head-ache and mental confusion that might last for minutes or hours—or just moments, if his plane spun out of control.

There was something very personal about shooting at another fellow, or being shot at by him, in a propeller-driven plane that is missing in today's jets. Planes had to come closer to one another in order to fire, not let go with guided missiles from miles away. And the planes were still slow enough that enemy pilots could see one another clearly. They could also see the results of their shooting up close. Often they had to fly through a blind-ing shower of sparks, all that remained of an enemy fighter that exploded in their path.

Photos of a ME-109 burning and plunging earthward taken from the gun-camera of an American fighter.

Then there were the close calls. A fighter pilot returned to base one day after a scrape with a FW-190. As he climbed out of the cockpit he began to rub his head. Everything was okay, he said, except for a splitting headache. The mechanics soon found the cause of his headache: a deep dent in the armor shield behind the pilot's head, the imprint of a Nazi bullet!

Fighter pilots were competitive by nature; competitive with the enemy, of course, but also with one another. "A fighter pilot must possess an inner urge to do combat," said Hubert Zemke, commander of the Fifty-sixth Fighter Group, nicknamed the "Wolfpack." Zemke knew what he was talking about. He shot down seventeen German planes himself, and his group had several high-scoring aces, being credited with destroying 1,006½ enemy planes.

Anyone who destroyed five enemy planes became an "ace," a very special warrior indeed. Fighter pilots competed to see who could gain the highest "kill" score. A "hot shot" might get another squadron member off an enemy's tail by shouting "Break!" over the radio; that's the signal to escape because an enemy is on your own tail. Once the other fellow broke, he'd move in to complete the kill and take the credit for himself.

The USAAF had dozens of aces, but only a handful of super aces. Major Richard I. Bong, its ace of aces and a Medal of Honor winner, downed forty Japanese planes while flying P-38s in the Southwest Pacific. Bong died in 1945 at the age of twenty-five, not in battle, but during a test flight in California.

Lieutenant Colonel Francis S. Gabreski was the

leading American ace in Europe with thirty-one victories. Majors Robert S. Johnson and Walter M. Mahurin followed Gabreski with twenty-eight and twenty-one victories apiece.

The team of Don S. Gentile and John T. Godfrey, flying Mustangs, downed some thirty-eight German planes. Goering was so annoyed at their daring that he said it would be worth losing two Luftwaffe squadrons to capture "the Italian Gentile and the Englishman Godfrey." Godfrey, already an ace before his twenty-first birthday, was captured but escaped and returned to duty.

America's aces had keen competition from the Luftwaffe's top scorers. Among these were the "heavy bomber specialists," nine pilots who downed between twenty and forty-four American bombers each. Another eight men were credited with shooting down between 100 and 158 USAAF and RAF fighters each. Among these was Adolf Galland with 104 victories.

It is lucky for the Allies that so much of Germany's best fighter talent was wasted in out-of-date planes. Imagine what someone like Galland might have done had he been able to fly jets earlier!

Germany was far ahead of the Allies in work on military jets. Ever since the 1930s it had been experimenting with planes which, it was hoped, would be able to fly faster than anything in the world.

Things went well until Hitler made one of the most important decisions of the war in the autumn of 1940. France had just fallen and it seemed only a matter of weeks until Great Britain would beg for peace. The war

The Messerschmitt ME-262 was the world's first jet fighter and might have changed the course of the war had not Hitler insisted that it be used as a bomber.

was won, he thought, so why waste manpower and materials on scientific research? He answered his own question by ordering a halt to any research that could not produce usable military results in four months. Among the projects shelved was the Messerschmitt ME-262 jet fighter.

Ploesti, Schweinfurt, and other big air battles in 1943 changed his mind and he allowed jet research to continue. Galland, who test-flew one of the first ME-262s, told how his plane shot through the air with a whistling sound. "It was as though the angels were pushing," he said.

Galland and the fighter pilots wanted jets to stop the Mustangs and regain control of the sky over Germany. This, they thought, was a sure thing; for at 540 miles an hour, and armed with four cannon and two dozen air-to-air rockets, the ME-262 was the deadliest flying machine ever built. Hitler disagreed. He wanted the plane as a "Blitz bomber" to punish English cities for the Allied air attacks. The problem was that it couldn't be *both* fighter and bomber; for turning it into a bomber meant making it carry extra weight, which would slow it down and throw away its speed advantage.

While the Germans wasted time arguing, the Allies acted. Time was growing short, and they had to break the Luftwaffe if the Normandy invasion was to take place as planned in the spring of 1944. German fighter factories were targeted during the "Big Week" from February 20–26. Every night RAF heavies went out alone to deliver their sledgehammer blows. During the day more than two thousand planes of the Eighth and Fifteenth Air Forces, escorted by Mustangs, took to the air. "Big Week" cost the USAAF 244 bombers and thirty-three fighters, but the enemy lost 692 of his precious fighters.

Early the next month, March 1944, Hap Arnold gave the order that became the Luftwaffe's death sentence. P-47s, P-38s, and P-51s equipped with drop-tanks were to change their tactics. Instead of sweeping the Luftwaffe out of the bombers' path, they were to rise in swarms and deliberately seek battle with the enemy fighters. Losses would be heavy but they could be made up with fresh planes and pilots waiting in the United States. The Germans would fall steadily behind until they had no air force left at all.

The best way to draw the Luftwaffe into this grinding machine was to strike Berlin. Not only was Berlin a center of war industry, but as Germany's capital and largest city it was also the pride of Hitler's "New Order." The RAF had attacked the "Big B" at night since the beginning of the war, but the Americans had not dared to go there in force in daylight.

On March 4, 1944, they went. Hundreds of Flying Fortresses and Mustangs filled the sky over the German capital. Goering, who by then was used to being called "Herr Meier," was shocked. As he saw the sleek fighters overhead, he knew that his country had lost the war.

Luftwaffe losses skyrocketed. From March to May, 1944, 2,442 fighters were lost in action and another fifteen hundred through accidents and other causes. Galland reported that each American attack was costing him about fifty planes, and these attacks were going on without a stop. "Things have gone so far," he warned in a secret report, "that the danger of the collapse of our (air) arm exists."

The Luftwaffe was in fact collapsing. Damaged factories might be fixed up and planes made somehow. But what about the men to fly these planes? Losses of experienced pilots ran far ahead of the numbers being graduated from training schools. The American fighter pilot of 1944 went into action with at least 450 hours of flying time behind him. The German pilot had to make do with only 150 hours. He couldn't, and soon the call came for another replacement.

Aviation gasoline was also disappearing. Beginning on May 12, 1944, the USAAF carried out mass attacks against Germany's factories that made oil and gasoline from coal. Oil production fell by more than half, and with it the amount of fuel needed to power Hitler's war machine. And since those factories also produced nitrogen and methanol, the basic chemicals in explosives, the armies began to run short of certain types of ammunition. Things became so bad that the explosive mixture in artillery shells had to be cut with rock salt.

Early on the morning of June 6, 1944 — D-Day morning — General Dwight D. ("Ike") Eisenhower, Supreme

Photograph taken by a mustang straffing a Luftwaffe fighter base at almost ground level, in preparation for D-Day.

Allied Commander in Europe, visited some American troops. Soon they would be joining a quarter-million others—Americans, Englishmen, Canadians—off the French beaches at Normandy to begin the liberation of Europe. They would be part of a five-thousand-ship fleet, the largest ever on the face of the earth.

These youngsters, Ike knew, were scared. *Anybody* would be scared, knowing what lay ahead. But to cheer them up a little he shared a piece of information: "You needn't worry about the air. If you see a plane it will be ours."

The air preparations for Operation OVERLORD had begun months before the first GI splashed ashore in France. The whole operation was to be covered by an aerial umbrella so wide and so thick that nothing would be able to stop the landings. By the time Allied air power had finished with them, the inventors of the *Blitzkrieg* would know that they had been blitzed by experts.

Airfields sprang up all over England. To the hundreds already built for the strategic bombers, another 168 bases were added. It seemed as though the whole country was being paved over with runways. Air Force men joked about how you could taxi a bomber the length and breadth of the island without scratching a wingtip.

The Allies had gathered over twelve thousand aircraft for OVERLORD: canvas-winged gliders, seaplanes, artillery spotters, transports, fighters, fighter-bombers, medium bombers, heavyweights, camera planes. Each had its own special role in the "show" Ike was preparing to put on. But whatever its job, every OVERLORD plane had black and white "invasion stripes" painted on its wings and fuselage. These would allow even the most cockeyed, trigger-happy GI or Tommy to recognize his own and hold his fire. Ike remembered the battles in North Africa in 1942, when American troops had shot down low-flying American planes by mistake.

The air fleets had three main jobs: destroy enemy shore defenses, prevent the Luftwaffe from interfering, and keep enemy reinforcements away from the beaches.

Normandy's shore defenses had been set up by one of Germany's best commanders. Field Marshal Erwin Rommel, the "Desert Fox," had been put in charge by Hitler himself. Rommel thought of everything: concrete forts to sweep the beach approaches with artillery fire, machine gun nests, millions of mines and metal-tipped spikes set below the water to rip open the bottoms of landing craft. Thanks to the camera planes most of these traps had been pinpointed. Those that could not be avoided would be blown up.

Nobody aboard the fleet anchored twelve miles offshore on D-Day morning could sleep. The hustle and bustle of last-minute preparations echoed through the ships. A stiff breeze made the water choppy. Those who were not too seasick to eat lined up at the doors of the steaming galleys for breakfast. Others checked their weapons for the hundredth time, or slipped a picture of the wife and kids into a waterproof envelope. Acres of cargo netting draped the ships' sides, waiting for the troops to climb down to the tiny landing boats bucking and bobbing in water below.

It was still dark when a strange sound began to be heard. It came slowly at first, like the buzzing of huge bumblebees in the distance. Then, as it built to a deafening roar, the bombers flew overhead. RAF heavies — Lancasters, Halifaxes, Sterlings — 1136 of them, came lumbering through the darkness to pound the shore defenses with nearly six thousand tons of high explosives. The first holes began to yawn in Hitler's famous "Atlantic Wall."

Nobody was asleep that morning either at USAAF bases in England. It had been a night of hurry and noise. As RAF earlybirds could be heard in the distance returning from Normandy, thousands of American planes began to warm their engines. They took off, formed tight Vee formations, and headed east toward the brightening horizon.

0550: Normandy. The troops of the first wave were already in the assault boats as the dawn began to break. Motors throbbed, belching puffs of white smoke. The tiny boats sprang forward and the dash to the shore began.

Spray-soaked men, seasick after hours of bouncing up and down in the light boats, turned pale and vomited into their helmets.

As the boats sped past the darkened shapes of the battleships towering above them, the heavens split and the sky became strangely lit. A sheet of flame leaped across the fleet from end to end, creating a man-made dawn. The naval bombardment had begun.

Dressed up in their D-Day best. A flight of Lockheed P-38 Lightnings wearing their invasion stripes head toward Normandy.

Battleships, cruisers, and destroyers lobbed shells at the shore defenses from their big guns. Among the biggest guns were those of the USS *Nevada,* burned and run aground at Pearl Harbor.

A river of hot steel rushed overhead at a rate of 200 tons of shells a minute. And the soaked, seasick thousands in the speeding boats looked up and cheered!

Suddenly another sound drowned out everything else. Ike was right. There were the planes.

At exactly 0600, and until 0630, when the first landing boat lowered its ramp, the USAAF would rake the shore defenses. The world had never seen such a sight before. Flying wingtip to wingtip, wave upon wave upon wave of planes soared over the fleet. There were seven thousand fighters and fighter-bombers, twenty-five hundred heavy bombers — ninety-five hundred planes, so many that it seemed hardly possible for the sky to hold them all at once.

The first of ten thousand tons of bombs rained down. And as they did, a tide of feeling rushed through the boats a thousand yards offshore. This was the air cover. Things would be okay now, maybe. Even if thousands of bombs missed their targets, they would pin Jerry down. Minefields would blow up and make lots of big, comfortable holes to hide in when they came ashore.

Other soldiers were watching too, only they had different feelings. They felt angry and disappointed. As the world was being smashed to pieces around their ears, German soldiers wondered: *"Wo ist die Luftwaffe?"* "Where is the Luftwaffe?"

Goering's once-mighty air force was no place where it could do them any good. D-Day found the Luftwaffe outclassed and outnumbered. Of the 119 fighters it had to cover Normandy, all except two were scattered across France for safety. These two, FW-190s, buzzed the beaches and fired a few shots before heading for safety at top speed. Where it really counted, the Allies outnumbered the enemy by *six thousand to one*.

After wondering about the Luftwaffe, Normandy's defenders might have asked another question: "Where are our reinforcements?" These were nowhere to be seen either, for part of the D-Day plan called for the USAAF to cut off the invasion area from the rest of France. No German soldier, tank, or gun was to be allowed to come within miles of the landing beaches.

During the two months before D-Day, the Eighth's heavy bombers and the Ninth's fighters, which had been moved to England from North Africa and reformed as a tactical air force, bombed every bridge and road connecting Normandy with the outside world. Railroads extending back hundreds of miles into Germany were given special attention, because flatcars are the only way to haul heavy armor quickly over long distances.

Whatever German reinforcements arrived in Normandy had to walk there. The story of the Second Panzer Division was repeated many times. When this unit was ordered to the front on June 7, its veteran troops expected to make mincemeat of the "soft" Allies. They had served in Russia and thought they knew everything anybody needed to know about fighting.

The Second Panzer's motorized columns coiled for miles along the French highway, without air cover. Everything seemed fine until they ran smack into a swarm of Thunderbolts. Before they knew what hit them the roadway was littered with splintered .88s and burning Tiger tanks.

The Second Panzer's commander wrote in his official report: "The Allies have total air supremacy. They bomb and shoot at anything that moves, even single vehicles and persons. Our territory is under constant observation. . . . The feeling of being powerless against the enemy's aircraft . . . has a paralyzing effect."

The Luftwaffe was too busy trying to save itself in the weeks after D-Day to bother about the army's needs. It was losing an average of 300 planes a week during the summer of 1944, and few replacements were coming in. From June to October thirteen thousand Luftwaffe men were killed, captured, or put out of action with wounds.

Galland found that his men were losing their fighting spirit. They were learning what it felt like to be the hunted instead of the hunter. Whenever their planes showed themselves, cruising American fighters swooped down with guns blazing. Their airfields were shot up and bombed in low-level hit-and-run raids. The Luftwaffe went into hiding in the forests, but whenever a plane was rolled out for takeoff the enemy appeared.

Meanwhile the invaders had grown into a million-man army and were preparing their breakout from Normandy. The jump-off point for the United States forces was the area around Saint-Lô and the operation was code-named COBRA. For the first time in history strategic bombers were to lend close-in support to infantry by laying a "bomb carpet" along five miles of front close to the American lines and right on top of the Germans' heads.

On the morning of July 25, some fifteen hundred Flying Fortresses and Liberators, followed by 750 me-

This B-26 Marauder medium bomber had an engine shot away during an attack on enemy positions guarding a French harbor.

dium bombers and fighters, dropped sixty thousand 100-pound bombs. The ground shook as they exploded like so many machine gun rounds. Some bombs came awfully close — too close for some GIs who were killed when some "shorts" fell into their foxholes.

When the smoke cleared the place looked like the face of the moon. Farmhouses and orchards looked as if a giant had stomped on them with hobnail boots. Telephone poles were splintered into matchsticks. German tank and artillery units simply disappeared, blown to nothing. Dead cows and dead Germans lay together in bomb craters.

A few days later General George S. Patton's Third Army bolted out of Normandy under its aerial umbrella. Patton's armored spearheads cut through the German defenses in great encircling movements aimed at trapping and wiping out as many enemy divisions as possible. For six days (August 13 to 19) British Typhoons and Ninth Thunderbolts strafed the retreating enemy. As far as the eye could see, tanks, trucks, artillery, and marching infantry jammed the roads. Allied pilots would seal off the front and rear of a column with a few bombs, then come screeching in low over the trapped survivors with machine guns and rockets.

German soldiers began to surrender to Allied airmen. A squadron of Thunderbolts caught 400 Jerries in the open. As they lined up for a strafing run the terrified footsoldiers waved white flags. The squadron reported its catch to Patton's headquarters and circled overhead until his troops came to collect the prisoners. An eighteen-year-old prisoner said his outfit's field kitchen had been wrecked and he hadn't eaten anything for four days.

Hitler's war machine was falling apart, although still far from destroyed. The madman in Berlin still had one more surprise up his sleeve. Along with their work on jets, his scientists had been working on a weapon that would again change war forever: long-range rockets.

During the spring of 1943, the British learned that the enemy was building "super weapons." Strange concrete structures shaped like a ski turned on its side began to spring up along the coasts opposite England; they seemed to be pointing toward London. Finally on D-Day plus seven, June 13, 1944, the world learned what the Nazis were up to. Their secret exploded in London in the shape of four V-1 "flying bombs."

The V-weapons (V for *Vergeltungswaffe,* vengeance weapons) were Hitler's last hope not of winning the war, but of killing a few more thousand innocent people before he died himself. The V-1 was an unmanned jet that carried a ton of explosives. When fired from its launching ramp, for that is what the ski-like structures were, it flew toward the target, crashing when its fuel ran out.

Until their launch sites were captured by the Allied armies, the Germans fired eight thousand V-1s at England, killing 6,184 people and wounding 17,981 others. Yet only a third of the "buzz-bombs" or "doodlebugs" got through. The V-1's weakness was its speed. It had a top speed of only 400 miles an hour, which allowed Mustangs and other fast fighters to catch up to it and shoot it down.

Then came the V-2. It had no nickname: it was too scary. The great-grandfather of today's Minutemen and Titans was forty-six feet long and weighed thirteen tons,

Nazi ''buzz-bomb'' or V-1 rocket flies over the rooftops of London.

with a one-ton TNT warhead. A liquid-fueled engine could hurl it fifty miles high, then send it diving earthward at four thousand miles an hour. You couldn't hear it. You couldn't see it. You knew it had arrived only after it was too late.

The only way to destroy a V-2 was to blow it up on its launching pad. Although the Allies blasted sites without letup, the RAF using even its monster Tallboy bombs, V-2s killed about twenty-five hundred Englishmen between September, 1944, and March, 1945. The United States was luckier: the Nazis were unable to carry out their plan of towing V-2s in containers across the Atlantic and firing them at New York and Boston.

That is not a problem anymore. Hitler told the truth when he said of the V-2: "Now and in the future, Europe and the world is too small for war. . . . War will become unbearable for the human race."

It had already become unbearable for the German people. Much hard fighting lay ahead, but the war's outcome was sure. In the east the Russians steadily forced the German armies back along a thousand-mile front. Whenever the Germans counterattacked in the west, as they did in the Battle of the Bulge in Belgium, they could keep up the pressure only as long as bad weather kept the Allied air forces grounded. Then the skies cleared, the planes took off, and they were forced back with heavy losses.

The strategic bombing continued without letup. Oil and gasoline practically disappeared, grounding the Luftwaffe's remaining planes and forcing the army to walk or use horses to pull its vehicles. The super highways of the Third Reich were lined for miles with tanks, trucks, and artillery left there when fuel ran out.

Americans examine a captured V-2 rocket at White Sands Proving Grounds, New Mexico, after the war.

By the beginning of March, 1945, United States and British armies were across the Rhine River and stabbing into the heart of Hitler's empire. Air targets were becoming very scarce. Mustang pilots, finding no more tanks to hit, began to chase individual soldiers across the fields. On April 16, Sir Arthur Harris called off large-scale RAF raids; four days later Tooey Spaatz did the same with the USAAF. By the end of the month Hitler had killed himself in a secret room buried deep under Berlin's flaming ruins and the Eighth began the move to the Pacific. Goering killed himself a year later after his trial by the Allies as a war criminal.

V-E Day (Victory-Europe) was officially announced on May 8, 1945. Celebration was in order.

That evening bonfires were lit, blackout curtains torn down, and lights turned on by the hundreds of thousands at every airbase in England. Colored flares rose into the sky like a July fourth celebration at airfields all over England. Over the public address system at a field an announcement would come in a stern voice: "There will be no more flares sent up from this base!" And right away hundreds more went skyward.

Searchlights all along the coast marked V for victory signs thousands of feet high.

Guns banged.

Sirens hooted.

Half a war was over.

Everyone knew that the celebration hadn't come cheaply. The RAF and USAAF dropped 2,775,000 tons of bombs on Europe during the Second World War. Delivering these bombs cost the British twenty-two thousand planes and 79,281 airmen; the Americans lost 18,418 planes and 79,625 airmen. Only the infantry paid a higher price for victory.

The enemy knew what those planes had cost *him*. Goering and Galland noted how Germany, having lost command of the air, had grabbed defeat from the arms of victory.

Which hurt the Nazi war effort most, RAF area night bombing or USAAF pinpoint daybombing? Again the enemy knew the answer. Field Marshal Erhard Milch, Goering's assistant, wrote in his diary: "The RAF bombers did us great damage, but the American daylight bombers cut out our heart." And so they did, to their honor and credit.

But a friend should have the last word. We remember that during those dark days of 1942, General Eaker said he hoped that when the Americans left the English would be glad they had come. By August, 1945, the last bomb groups were gone. After seeing some of the boys safely into the air, the people from a town near one of the bases walked back to the airfield.

They strolled home across the deserted runway, no one speaking, each person wrapped in his or her own thoughts. Later a woman spoke for all: "For more than two years (the Yanks) lived in and were part of our countryside, and we missed them sincerely when they were gone."

5

The Pacific Boils Over

Banzai! Banzai! Banzai! ("May the Emperor live ten thousand years!")

Again and again the men's voices rose in high-pitched screams. Samurai swords flashed, slicing the air as the blue-uniformed officers danced around waving them over their heads.

It was the morning of December 7, 1941, and moments before the carrier *Akagi,* flagship of the Pearl Harbor task force, had signaled Imperial Japanese Navy headquarters: "Surprise attack successful!" Soon Radio Tokyo's English-language broadcast told the world that the United States Pacific Fleet had been "destroyed to pieces."

Japan's sailors and airmen had turned the American battle fleet into a heap of twisted junk in less than an hour. Eighteen mighty warships were sunk or badly damaged. One lucky dive-bomber pilot dropped his bomb down the smokestack of the battleship *Arizona,* blowing her boilers and ammunition rooms skyhigh.

American air power nearly disappeared in the Pacific. While Japanese dive-bombers and torpedo planes were plastering "Battleship Row," their fighters went for the airfields where they found the planes neatly lined up on the runways. Of Pearl Harbor's 394 planes, 188 were destroyed and 159 damaged.

The Japanese killed nearly three thousand Americans that morning at a cost to themselves of fifty-five men, twenty-nine planes, and a few midget submarines. It was a victory to be "proud" of.

Yet Pearl Harbor was only a warmup for the warriors of the Rising Sun. In the following days and weeks Japanese forces captured the American bases at Guam and Wake Island; a large army invaded the Philippines and slowly destroyed General Douglas MacArthur's army in the jungles of the Bataan peninsula. America's friends suffered as badly when the Japanese overran the Dutch East Indies, drove the British out of Hong Kong and Burma, and captured their fortress city of Singapore in Malaya.

Everything had gone so smoothly that the Japanese themselves were surprised. Victory, they said, proved the justice of their cause. The Japanese home islands have little living space, many people, and few natural resources. Much of the nation's rice and all of its raw materials — oil, rubber, tin, nickel, etc. — must be brought from overseas and is controlled by foreigners.

Prime Minister Tojo, and the other warlords who ruled Japan for the Emperor Hirohito, wanted to capture the rich lands of Asia. If they could do this, their country would always have all the raw materials it needed. And they hoped to keep what they had taken by setting up naval and air bases on the chains of islands that stretch across the Pacific for thousands of miles from Japan. Once this defense line was set up, they believed no enemy could harm Japan. Only the fleet at Pearl Harbor stood in the way, and it was finished off in an hour.

One important military man alone wasn't so sure that this plan would work. He was a strange person, this doubter. He had a number for a first name, "Fifty-six," given him because that was his father's age when he was born. Short and stocky, he looked like a pint-sized wrestler. He loved to play poker, watch baseball games, and stand on his head for hours at a time. His name was Admiral Isoroku Yamamoto, Commander in Chief of the Japanese Imperial Navy.

Yamamoto was a genius. He knew ships, knew airplanes, and knew that only the two together could control the Pacific Ocean. He also knew and liked Americans. He had lived in the United States for several years as a student at Harvard University. During those years he learned that even though the United States might seem weak, its wealth in people and things was so great that it could shake off any defeat.

Yamamoto obeyed when his superiors ordered him to plan the attack on Pearl Harbor. But he also gave them a warning: "If it is necessary to fight, in the first six months to a year of war against the United States and England

"Old Leatherface," Brigadier General Claire Lee Chennault (right) talks with "Hap" Arnold during a visit to a Flying Tiger air base in China.

I will run wild. I will show you an uninterrupted succession of victories. But I must also tell you that if the war be prolonged for two or three years I have no confidence in our ultimate victory."

Some Americans had been fighting their own private war against Japan even before Yamamoto completed his plans for Pearl Harbor. Their leader was a thin, wiry man of fifty-one named Claire Lee Chennault. They were called the American Volunteer Group, or "Flying Tigers" for short.

Chennault had been one of the Army Air Corps' best fighter pilots until his hearing began to fail and he had to retire as a captain in 1937. Unemployed, with a wife and four children to support, Chennault didn't know what to do until a Chinese officer visited him. China had just been invaded by Japan and needed an air force. Could Chennault build one?

Could he! *General* Chennault became a one-man air force by himself, shooting down at least forty Japanese planes in old, beaten-up crates that should have been scrapped years ago. Still China was losing the air war, for Chennault was only a man. He could not make modern warplanes with his bare hands, or train skilled pilots overnight. These were available only at home.

FDR understood the problem. He wanted a strong China to balance the power of Japan in Asia. But at that time America was still at peace with Japan, and allowing pilots and planes to fight for China would be seen in Tokyo as an unfriendly act.

But FDR wanted to help China, and on April 15, 1941, he quietly signed an order allowing Army, Navy, and Marine Corps pilots to quit the service to join Chennault's American Volunteer Group. He also allowed the Chinese air force to buy a hundred Curtis P-40 Tomahawk fighters.

Chennault's men volunteered for different reasons. Some wanted adventure, like the pioneers who once crossed the Great Plains. Others saw China's fight as a fight for freedom everywhere. And the pay was good. At a time when most American workers were glad to earn $25 a week, his pilots earned $600 a month plus $500 for each Japanese plane shot down.

By July, 1941, Chennault and 150 pilots and mechanics were getting ready to meet the enemy. One day someone saw magazine pictures of RAF fighter planes with blood-red mouths and rows of shark teeth painted on their radiators. Since the Japanese believed in evil spirits, why not paint this design together with an evil eye on the P-40 and scare the daylights out of them? Another member of the group drew a design of a tiger with tiny wings jumping through a V for victory sign. The "Flying Tigers" were born.

Had Chennault sent his Tigers into battle as soon as possible, they would have become dead pussycats in no time. The Japanese Mitsubishi S-OO, or Zero, was the best fighter plane in Asia in 1941. At a top speed of 317 miles an hour it was not very fast. But it could climb to sixteen thousand feet in six minutes and make a 180-degree turn in under six seconds. To dogfight the Zero with any American plane of the time was to commit suicide.

Chennault knew the P-40 was too heavy to fight the Zero on its own terms. Yet the Japanese could be beaten, because the Zero had two weaknesses. Maneuverability had been bought at the price of safety. The Japanese had given up armor plate to save weight, and the plane lacked self-sealing gas tanks. A few hits with .50-caliber slugs

Curtis P-40 Tomahawk fighters fly across the mountains near Chunking, China, on their way to enemy targets.

and the Zero would break apart like a cheap toy or burn like a torch. And the P-40 carried eight "big fifties."

Chennault taught the Tigers never to go one-on-one with a Zero, but to fight in pairs. That way they'd be able to look after one another and take advantage of their combined firepower. They were to attack from above, making the most of the P-40's weight and teriffic diving speed. Never, he warned, *NEVER* "mix it up" with a Zero after a pass. "Hit hard, break clean, and get into position for another pass."

Chennault's tactics worked. Even though outnumbered by better than ten to one, the Tigers still thought the odds were "even." The Japanese didn't: they thought the odds unfair. One moment sixty "Betty" two-engined bombers and forty Zeros would be flying along without a care in the world. Next moment eight or ten of those ferocious looking P-40s were tearing through their formation like so many tiger sharks. Zeros spun earthward in flames. Betties fell apart in showers of sparks. The formation turned tail and headed home at top speed.

The Tigers liked to ambush Japanese convoys on narrow mountain roads. They attacked in line fifteen feet off the ground, leaving a trail of burning vehicles and dead soldiers. After one raid the Chinese troops who had watched the whole thing from across the valley stood up and waved their hats as the Tigers roared overhead on the way back to their base. "Old Leatherface," as the Chinese called Chennault, and his *Fei Weing* (Flying Tigers) were earning their pay. The Japanese were so angered by these hit-and-run attacks that they broadcast a radio warning: unless the Tigers fought "fairly," they would be shot on the spot when captured. The Tigers payed no attention to this warning, for they had seen more than a few of their buddies machine-gunned as they floated down under their parachutes.

The Flying Tiger story ended when their contracts with the Chinese government ended on July 4, 1942. A few stayed on to help Chennault in his new post as commander of the United States Fourteenth Air Force. Most returned home for some rest before reenlisting.

The Flying Tigers chalked up a record that would make any group of air fighters jealous. During six months of combat they were officially credited with downing 297 enemy planes, although the total was probably closer to 600. Besides these they cost the Japanese at least fifteen hundred airmen and uncounted infantry, tanks, trucks, and supplies.

Admiral Yamamoto had better things to think about than the Flying Tigers, for he knew that Pearl Harbor was not as successful as he had intended. The three ships he most wanted to destroy were not in port when his planes struck, but at sea. And as long as *Enterprise, Lexington,* and *Saratoga* were afloat, Japan could never feel safe. Somewhere out there, hidden in the wide watery wastes of the Pacific Ocean, American aircraft carriers were hunting.

Some were on a secret mission dreamed up by, of all people, a submarine officer, Captain Francis S. Low. Why not bring the war to Tokyo itself? Low wondered. Why not have Army bombers flying from an aircraft carrier do a Pearl Harbor in reverse? The Navy passed the idea to Hap Arnold, who asked Colonel James H. Doolittle to think it over.

At forty-seven, "Jimmy" Doolittle had spent most

of his life doing the impossible. He had set a record when he flew across the United States in twelve hours and was the first person to land a plane blindfolded. He jumped at the idea of a Tokyo raid.

Doolittle's plan was for sixteen twin-engined B-25 medium bombers to take off from a carrier before nightfall 400 miles from the Japanese capital. They would attack in darkness and then head west, landing in free China early the next morning.

This was easier said than done. A B-25 with a five-man crew and four 500-pound bombs needed plenty of room for takeoff. But the flight deck of the carrier *Hornet,* the one chosen for the mission, was only about 480 feet long. Would it be long enough?

Doolittle thought so, if his volunteer crews were well-trained. For many weeks he put them through their paces at Elgin Field, Florida. After hundreds of tries, they became experts in taking off in the shortest possible space.

Doolittle's crews and planes were loaded aboard the *Hornet* at San Francisco. *Hornet,* nicknamed the "Blue Ghost," and her escorts put to sea under sealed orders. Only after they had sailed under the Golden Gate and the California coast slipped out of sight did *Hornet*'s skipper, Captain Marc A. Mitscher, read the order over the loudspeakers and flash them by blinker to the other ships. Cheers echoed back across the water as the crews read the lights. Meanwhile, another task force was steaming out of Pearl Harbor to meet Mitscher's little fleet. Leading this force was Admiral William F. Halsey, Jr., aboard the *Enterprise.*

As the combined task force neared Japan, airmen took part in a strange ceremony. United States Navy officers who had received Japanese medals for merit during the peace years turned them in after Pearl Harbor, asking that they be "returned" with the first bombs sent to Tokyo. Doolittle was glad to oblige and posed for photographs as he wired them to a 500-pounder. The flyers then chalked messages on the bombs: *"I don't want to set the world on fire, only Tokyo,"* and *"You'll get a BANG out of this!"*

Snafu. Before dawn on the morning of April 18, 1942, the carriers' patrol planes sighted and sank a Japanese ship. Had it reported the Americans' position? Halsey and Doolittle had no way of knowing. All they knew was that the mission would have to begin immediately and in broad daylight, even though the flight would be longer than planned.

"Army pilots, man your planes!" boomed the voice on *Hornet*'s bullhorn.

Navy men used mechanical donkeys to push and pull the B-25s into position on the ship's deck. Although the gas gauges read "full," they rocked the planes to break any bubbles that might have formed in the wing tanks, and then topped the tanks. A few extra pints might make the difference between life and death, now that they had to fly an extra 150 miles.

A stiff breeze was blowing as Mitscher turned *Hornet*'s bow into the wind. The carrier heaved and rolled, rose and fell, in the waves. The deck became slippery as green water broke over its ramps.

Everyone held his breath as Doolittle raced his

engines faster and faster. Then the B-25, its left wing jutting over *Hornet*'s port (left) side, shot forward into the wind. Once airborne, Doolittle circled the ship, zooming straight down above the white line painted in the center of her deck. The ship shuddered with the sailors' hoarse cheers.

Soon all sixteen planes, eighty men, were winging toward Japan. The enemy was taken completely by surprise. As the planes flew low over Tokyo, the crews could see the crowds in the streets below waving at them. (The old Army Air Corps insignia was a blue circle with a white star and red ball in the center, which looked like

Comrades in arms. Captain Marc Mitcher of the U.S.S. *Hornet* meets with Air Force Colonel "Jimmy" Doolittle and his crews before their raid on Tokyo.

Tokyo-bound. One of Doolittle's B-25 bombers lifts off *Hornet*'s deck in the first raid on the Japanese capital.

the Japanese rising sun emblem ("meatball") from the distance.) Radio Tokyo was explaining why Japan was the only country at war free from the danger of attack. It went on to say that it was a fine day in Tokyo, with the Festival of the Cherry Blossoms in full swing. Just then you could hear the air-raid sirens as the broadcaster's microphone picked them up from outside the studio.

Steel mills, gasoline refineries, rail yards, a battleship under construction, and other military targets exploded as Doolittle's planes flew over them. *Only* military targets were hit. Doolittle's raiders never touched a civilian. They passed by the most tempting target of all, the Imperial Palace with Emperor Hirohito inside, without dropping a bomb or firing a shot.

Thirty seconds over Tokyo; that's how long the whole raid took. Then came the hard job of getting away. All the planes escaped safely. Japanese fighters rose to meet the invaders but missed them; antiaircraft fire was a joke. Nature was the real enemy, for Doolittle's planes ran into a storm and had to buck strong headwinds. Night was falling, and so were the needles in their gas gauges, when most of the crews bailed out over China. Chinese villagers found them, cared for the wounded, and helped them escape to free China. Eight other crewmen were captured by the Japanese.

The Japanese military were angry. They had promised Hirohito that Japan would never be bombed, and now they had been embarrassed. Admiral Yamamoto was so ashamed that he locked himself in his room and refused to come out.

The chief of Tokyo's antiaircraft defenses was ordered to kill himself. He did. Then every Chinese village that had helped the Americans was destroyed and every man, woman, and child killed. Over two hundred fifty thousand Chinese died for being kind to Doolittle's men.

The captured Americans were put on trial for "inhuman acts" against "schools and hospitals." All eight were beaten and tortured before the court found them guilty and sentenced them to death. Three were executed, while the others received "mercy" and sentences of life in prison.

Doolittle had really scared the Japanese high command. Where had his planes come from? Could others come after them? President Roosevelt offered no help. He announced that they had taken off from Shangri-La, the never-never land of *Lost Horizon,* a popular novel of the time.

Tokyo now decided that it needed more "antiair-raid insurance." And the best insurance was to put more miles of ocean between Japan and United States airpower. Once completed, it was hoped that Japan's outer defense ring would run from the Aleutian Islands in the North Pacific near Alaska, down to Midway in the Central Pacific within range of Pearl Harbor, and across the Southwest Pacific toward Australia. This plan brought out the aircraft carriers of both countries in force and touched off the battles of the Coral Sea and Midway.

The first blow fell near the islands along the sea road to Australia. Although poor in natural resources, the "new" islands of the Southwest Pacific are nature's stepping stones to the island continent of Australia. New Ireland and New Britain in the Bismarck Sea lie just north of New Guinea; and New Guinea is less than two hundred miles north of Australia. If Australia fell, United States supply lines would be cut and it would lose its main base for a counterattack in that part of the world.

Tokyo had had its eyes on these islands for many years. Spy ships disguised as fishing boats had mapped the area and learned that it was practically undefended by the British and Australians. Japanese forces moved in during the weeks after Pearl Harbor and built great naval and air bases at Rabaul on New Britain and Kavieng on New Ireland. New Guinea was next.

But here's where the Japanese ran into trouble. The town of Port Moresby on New Guinea's southern coast opposite Australia had been turned into an Allied base. Capturing it would unlock Australia's back door. Unfortunately Port Moresby is on the far side of the Owen Stanley Mountains. No general would march troops over these jungle-covered thirteen thousand-foot peaks if he could reach this place by ship.

The Imperial Navy had plenty of ships. All it had to do was sail from Rabaul into the Coral Sea, loop around the New Guinea coast, and land troops near Port Moresby. Only a tiny United States–Australian fleet under Rear Admiral Frank Fletcher stood in the way; and, of course, carriers *Lexington* and *Yorktown,* known affectionately to their crews as "Lady Lex" and "Yorkie."

The Coral Sea is one of the most beautiful bodies of water in the world. Ocean storms usually pass it by. Its waters are warm and so clear that you can see coral gardens in the shallows near its islands and along the thousand miles of Australia's Great Barrier Reef. The sky above is a cloudless, deep blue.

This corner of Paradise became a battleground when the opposing fleets fought on May 7 and 8, 1942. The Battle of the Coral Sea was special. Great warships exploded and sank, but not once did they fire a gun at one another. They never even *saw* one another. Planes did all the fighting with machine guns, bombs, and torpedoes.

The ships' guns were used only to put up curtains of anti-aircraft fire.

Fliers from *Lexington* and *Yorktown* picked off seven Japanese ships, including the light carrier *Shoho*. "Scratch one flattop!" the dive bomber leader shouted excitedly into his radio. At last, after five months of war, the Americans had sunk an enemy vessel larger than a "tin can," a destroyer.

Japanese planes scored also, sinking an American oiler and a destroyer. Then seventy planes dived on the carriers. One bomb went through *Yorktown*'s flight deck, starting fires that were quickly brought under control. But the Pacific Fleet let the Japanese think "Yorkie" had been lost; sometimes it is good to seem weaker than you really are.

Lexington wasn't so lucky. Two torpedoes tore into her port side, while bombs started fires on her main deck. The fires spread and terrific explosions began to rock the ship belowdecks. Men were thrown through the air by the force of the explosions. Steel doors twisted on their hinges, creating openings that allowed air to circulate freely in the "airtight" compartments.

Damage Control fought to save the ship, but it didn't have a chance. As the steel walls heated up, fuel oil and gasoline evaporated, forming vapor pockets that exploded into clouds of flame. It was only a matter of time before the fires reached piles of bombs and the ten tons of torpedo warhead explosive stored belowdecks.

The crewmen took the abandon ship order calmly, although they knew the Coral Sea was infested with man-eating sharks. They lined up their shoes on the flight deck and silently waited their turn to go down the ropes to the rescue boats or into the water. Some filled their helmets with ice cream from the ship's stores and ate it until their turn came at the ropes. Luckily no sharks were around, probably because the explosions frightened them away.

Planes crowd the flight deck of the carrier U.S.S. *Lexington* after a raid on an enemy-held island in the Pacific.

As night fell, *Lexington*'s sides glowed a deep cherry-red. She shook with explosions. Fire swept the length of her deck. But she wouldn't sink. Her fires, though, lighted the sky, acting as a beacon for the enemy.

And so she died at the hands of those who loved her. A United States destroyer sent four torpedoes into her starboard side. She began to settle into the water, hissing and coughing smoke as the waves slowly washed over her.

Her crewmen on the rescue ships stood at the rails and wept. One murmured: "There she goes. She didn't turn over. She's going down with her head up. Dear old *Lex*. A lady to the last!"

Yet she hadn't gone for nothing. For at that very moment the Japanese admiral was turning his fleet around and setting a course back to Rabaul. Never again would New Guinea be threatened from the sea.

Admiral Yamamoto meanwhile was forming a plan to finish the job begun at Pearl Harbor and knock the United States out of the war in a single battle. A decoy force would invade the Aleutian Islands, coaxing Admiral Chester W. Nimitz, commander of the Pacific Fleet, into sending part of his fleet on a wild goose chase to the north. But the real attack would come at Midway, two coral specks in the ocean twenty-three hundred miles east of Japan and eleven hundred miles northwest of Pearl Harbor. Yamamoto hoped to use Midway as bait to lure Nimitz into a battle he couldn't win. Once Nimitz set out to protect Midway, Yamamoto's fleet would crush him like a steamroller. Midway would then be turned into an advance base from which to protect Japan or to attack Hawaii and the Pacific coast of the United States itself.

Yamamoto sailed on May 27, 1942, with the largest battle fleet ever seen in the Pacific Ocean. A screen of sixty-five destroyers fanned out in front of the main body of eleven battleships, twenty-two heavy cruisers, twenty-one submarines, and eighty transports. Three hundred miles ahead Admiral Chuichi Nagumo sailed with the same carrier strike force he had led against Pearl Harbor.

His four fleet carriers — *Hiru, Soryu, Kaga, Akagi* — could put 275 planes into the air.

The Japanese played games and sang songs as their ships barreled through the water. They might not have been so happy had they known what Nimitz knew. The American admiral had MAGIC on his side. United States military intelligence had broken the top-secret Japanese code and was reading all of Yamamoto's radio messages. MAGIC, the cover name for the broken code, told Nimitz exactly what Yamamoto was up to in the Aleutians and at Midway.

Nimitz turned Midway into a pincushion of antiaircraft guns and shore defense guns manned by United States Marines. Every warship he could scrape together was at sea: eight cruisers, fourteen destroyers, twelve submarines. They weren't much, compared to Yamamoto's fleet, but Nimitz knew the enemy's plans, and that was worth a lot.

The backbone of Nimitz's fleet was the carriers *Enterprise, Hornet,* and *Yorktown.* That "Yorkie" was able to fight so soon after Coral Sea was also "magical." Hundreds of shipyard workers at Pearl Harbor worked around the clock to make her seaworthy. Welders wedged themselves into tight spaces belowdecks and in 120-degree heat leaned over the sputtering sparks and blue flashes of their torches. Instead of the three months needed to make "Yorkie" ready for combat, they gave Nimitz back his ship in forty-eight hours.

The Battle of Midway began early in the morning on June 4, 1942. Admiral Nagumo drew first blood with a 100-plane strike on Midway to soften it up for invasion.

But the island's defenses were harder than he thought, and his air commander on the scene radioed for a second strike to finish the job.

Nagumo now made the worst mistake of his life. He had kept a reserve of ninety-three planes armed with armor-piercing bombs and torpedoes in case United States ships were sighted. He hadn't the foggiest idea of where Nimitz's ships were, what kind of ships he had, or if he had any ships at all. But since his scouts reported no Americans in sight, he ordered the reserve rearmed with antipersonnel and incendiary bombs for a second visit to Midway.

As the rearming began, a scout reported a large formation of American ships to the northeast. Surprised by this news, and knowing that the Midway strike formations would be overhead soon and low on fuel, Nagumo ordered the reserve lowered to the hangar decks to be armed again for a sea attack. His decks cleared, he turned his ships into the wind and began to land the homecoming planes.

This operation was almost over when United States Navy torpedo planes arrived. A group of fifteen came in low, without fighter cover. Nagumo's antiaircraft guns opened up, filling the sky with beautiful colors. Each ship's antiaircraft shells burst with a different color — blue, yellow, pink, red, white, purple — to help the gun crews tell how they were shooting. The torpedo planes that weren't wiped out by these beautiful colors were shot down by the Zeros of Nagumo's combat air patrols.

Another torpedo squadron came in, losing ten out of fourteen planes. One American plane headed straight for *Akagi*'s bridge, overshot it by inches, and spun into the sea off the port side. Admiral Kusaka, Nagumo's chief of staff, couldn't believe his eyes. The "cowardly" Americans were as daring as any Samurai warrior of ancient Japan. Kusaka said a silent prayer for a brave enemy.

The torpedo planes' sacrifice doomed the Japanese carriers. For trailing them by two minutes were two squadrons of Dauntless dive-bombers under Lieutenant Commander Clarence W. McClusky, air group commander of *Enterprise*.

The Japanese combat air patrols were still skimming the waves and unable to regain altitude so quickly after downing the torpedo planes. All of Nagumo's torpedo bombers were back on their flight decks, together with their fighter escorts, when he turned the carriers into the wind again. In five minutes the sky would swarm with Japanese planes. Just then, at 1024 hours, as the launch order came from *Akagi*'s bridge, McClusky's thirty-seven planes began to dive.

Down below at that instant a lookout screamed "Helldivers!" Hell broke loose as bombs crashed among the planes crowding *Kaga*'s flight deck. The planes, their bombs and torpedoes, and their gasoline tanks exploded like a string of firecrackers. The BOOM . . . BOOM . . . BOOM of the bombs mixed with the quick BANG, BANG, BANG as the overheated machine gun bullets went off, mowing down crewmen as they tried to fight the wall of fire that rolled across the ship's deck.

It was the same on *Akagi* and *Soryu*. Commander Mitsuo Fuchida, the Japanese Naval Air Force officer who had led the first planes over Pearl Harbor, saw everything from *Akagi*'s bridge. "Looking about, I was horrified at the destruction that had been wrought in a

matter of seconds. There was a huge hole in the flight
deck just behind the amidship elevator. The elevator itself, twisted like molten glass, was dropping into the
hangar. Deck plates reeled up . . . Planes stood tail
up, belching livid flame and jet-black smoke. Reluctant
tears streamed down my face as I watched the fires
spread."

At 1024 Japanese sailors were rejoicing as the last
American torpedo plane crashed in flames. Six minutes
later three of their carriers were burning wrecks. War's
changes and chances are swift and terrible.

Only *Hiryu* remained, for the moment. Her planes
found *Yorktown* and seriously wounded her; she was
torpedoed by a Japanese submarine and sunk later. But
Hiryu's pilots didn't enjoy their victory for long. Dive
bombers from *Enterprise,* plus *Yorktown* planes that had
landed on the "Big E's" deck, found *Hiryu* and sent her
under.

The gambler had staked everything on one card —
and lost. Yamamoto had lost four of the best ships in the
Imperial Navy together with all their planes and pilots,
plus forty-eight hundred seamen and two heavy cruisers.
He locked himself in his cabin on the battleship *Yamato*
and sulked all the way home.

Yet he should have been at least a little satisfied. He
had been right from the beginning. He had promised to
"run wild" if forced to fight, and he did. Then, three days
short of six months after Pearl Harbor, his luck ran out.
United States Navy carrier planes would see that it never
returned.

6

Island Hopping

We know today that Coral Sea and Midway were turning points in the Pacific war. Never again would Japan have a victory, or the United States a defeat. But only a very brave person, or a very foolish one, could have said this in the summer of 1942. The Japanese were still making the moves. They, not the Americans, decided where to go and when to go there.

After Midway the high command in Tokyo decided to call off the advance eastward across the Pacific. Instead Japanese forces would strike south again from Rabaul toward Australia in a two-sided air-sea-land attack.

The first attack was aimed at Port Moresby. If this key Allied base couldn't be taken the easy way, by sea, then the Japanese knew how to take it the hard way. On

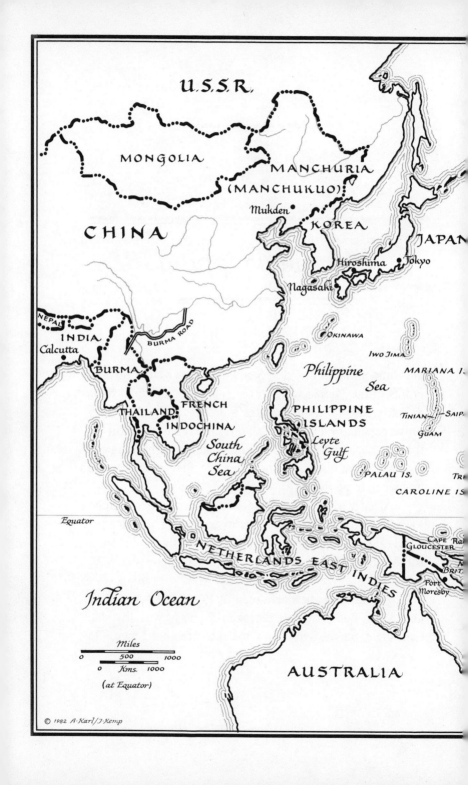

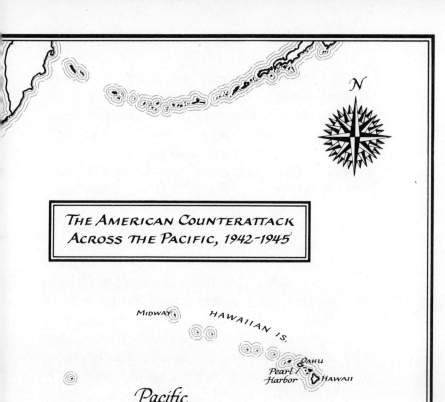

N

THE AMERICAN COUNTERATTACK
ACROSS THE PACIFIC, 1942-1945

MIDWAY HAWAIIAN IS.

OAHU
Pearl
Harbor HAWAII

Pacific

Ocean

NIWETOK

KWAJALEIN

MAKIN GILBERT
TARAWA IS.

BOUGAINVILLE
SOLOMON IS.

GUADALCANAL

Coral

Sea

July 21, 1942, a large army from Rabaul was landed at Buna on New Guinea's north coast. Moving inland, the troops began to climb the Kokoda Trail. This narrow jungle track led through a little-known 6700-foot gap in the Owen Stanley Mountains and ended in the jungle a few miles behind Port Moresby. Soon it would be known as the "Bloody Trail."

At about the same time Japanese forces began to occupy the Solomon Islands. Lying a few hundred miles east of New Guinea, the Solomons are a double chain of jungle islands seven hundred miles long and separated by a channel called "The Slot." As part of their earlier drive into the Coral Sea, the Japanese had taken Tulagi and its fine harbor. Then, late in June, they began to build an airstrip on a nearby island that almost no one had ever heard of. Soon planes from that airstrip would be ranging over the Coral Sea to cut the sea lanes to Australia. The island is called Guadalcanal.

The Allies would either have to stop the Japanese in the Owen Stanleys and on Guadalcanal or lose Australia and the whole Southwest Pacific along with it.

FDR had ordered General Douglas MacArthur to escape from the Philippines and continue the war from Australia. On April 18, 1942, as Jimmy Doolittle's planes were heading for Tokyo, the sixty-two year old general took command of all United States forces in Australia and the Southwest Pacific.

MacArthur knew the value of air power, believing that there was no way to turn back the Japanese without it. Yet he did not like airmen. They had let him down in the Philippines, he thought, by having all their planes parked in the open at Clark Field when the Japanese attacked a few hours after Pearl Harbor. MacArthur's whole air force was wiped out in a few minutes. How could he count on these "losers" to help him win in New Guinea?

MacArthur's opinion of airmen changed when Lieutenant General George C. Kenney arrived to take over the Fifth Air Force in July 1942. Short and stocky, Kenney at fifty-three was as tough as they come. He was a professional soldier who had fought in Europe during the First World War and had been shot down by the

General Douglas MacArthur, commander of U.S. forces in the Southwest Pacific, with General Carl (Tooey) Spaatz (left) and General George Kenney.

Germans. Not one for wasting words, he let you know what he thought in short sentences that hit like blackjacks.

Kenney believed that tanks and big guns had their place in Europe and North Africa, where the ground was level and hard, but not in the jungles of New Guinea; there the artillery must fly. His aim was simply "to own the air over New Guinea" so that MacArthur's troops could push the Japanese back over the Kokoda Trail and into the sea. Owning the air, he said, meant more than controlling the sky over the battlefield for a while: "It means air control so supreme that the birds have to wear our Air Force insignia. Wrecking the enemy's ground installations does not mean just softening them up. It means taking out everything he has — aerodromes, guns, bunkers, troops."

That was a tall order, but Kenney knew what he wanted and how to get it. Within days of taking over, he fired all officers who had not fought well in the past. Then he began to use planes in ways that old-timers thought crazy. When MacArthur needed to rush fresh troops to Port Moresby, Kenney told him not to waste time with ships. "Give me five days and I'll ship the whole damned U.S. Army to New Guinea by air."

Kenney was as good as his word. He airlifted thousands of troops in a few days. He even airlifted their two-and-a-half-ton trucks. Since these were too large to fit into a transport plane, he had them cut in half with blowtorches and welded together when they arrived at Port Moresby.

Nothing seemed too hard for this hardbitten little man. If he could airlift troops, he could also drop them by parachute behind enemy lines. MacArthur wasn't so sure about this, but let him try anyhow. As the troops fluttered safely to the ground, MacArthur, watching the scene from his own B-17 named *"Bataan,"* was so happy that he began to jump up and down.

MacArthur grew to like Kenney as he did few others. Throwing a friendly arm around the airman's shoulders, he said: "George, you were born three hundred years too late. You're just a natural-born pirate." Then he gave Kenney a nickname that stayed with him the rest of his life: "Buccaneer."

Kenney loved the nickname as much as his men loved using it. Between the general and his men there was always respect and trust. Kenney called his flyers the "Kids," because they were so young. When his Kids got into trouble, he defended them, although he might chew them out later in private.

But the Japanese hated Kenney because they feared him. Like Chennault, he had some of the best fighter pilots in the USAAF under his command. They were the best and they let everyone know it. They made it a habit to operate on the same radio frequency as the Japanese in order to trade insults with them on the air and to challenge them to come up and fight.

The Fifth Air Force's most famous pilot was Major Richard Bong: "Bing Bong" the others called him. Kenney had learned about him in the States, when a housewife complained that some lunatic pilot had come in so low with a P-38 that he blew her clothes off the line. Kenney liked that sort of daring; he had almost been thrown out of the Air Service in 1917 for "stunting"

Some of General George C. Kenney's "parafrags" drift down toward a Japanese bomber parked under a layer of branches for camouflage. Parafrags were small fragmentation bombs with supersensitive fuses attached to parachutes that allowed low-flying bombers to escape the blast of their own bombs.

under the bridges that span New York's East River. Bong became the USAAF's all-time ace with forty victories. Yet he was an awful marksman. He just couldn't shoot straight. He destroyed enemy planes by flying so close to them that even he couldn't miss.

Although Kenney's days as a fighter pilot were past, he had plenty of tricks to share with his Kids. One of his special interests was low-level bombing. Bombing close to the ground had always been risky, because bombs fell so fast and their explosions were so powerful that they might blow the planes that dropped them to pieces if they couldn't get away fast enough.

Kenney invented the "parafrag," or parachute fragmentation bomb, to solve this problem. The parafrag was a twenty-five-pound fragmentation bomb attached to a small parachute. A medium bomber could fly at tree-top level, drop its parafrags, and have plenty of time to escape as they drifted down. The nose of each bomb had a very sensitive fuse that went off at the slightest touch; even a leaf would kick it off. The explosion sent a thousand steel splinters flying in every direction. Each splinter traveled at twice the speed of a high-powered rifle bullet and could go through a two-inch piece of wood.

Another invention was the "Kenney Cocktail." This was not a drink but a 100-pound bomb case filled with white phosphorous instead of TNT. White phosphorous burns in the air, and when a phosphorous bomb hit something hard it burst, shooting out flaming streamers 150 feet in every direction. Water will not put out a white phosphorous fire, nor will covering it with earth. Anyone or anything touched by it is lost.

One of Kenney's assignments was to stop fresh Japanese troops from reaching New Guinea by sea. Sending Flying Fortresses and Liberators to do the job was a waste of bombs. A ship can move quickly and cut a zig-zag course. By the time bombs land from twenty-five thousand feet, the ship has moved out of the way. High-altitude bombers never sank a ship during the whole of the Pacific war.

Kenney found a way for low-flying two-engine bombers to destroy enemy shipping. It is called "skip bombing." Every youngster who has played with flat stones near a lake knows how to skip-bomb. A stone thrown at a shallow angle will "skip" along the water's surface several times before losing power and sinking. So will a bomb when dropped from a low-flying plane. The bomb skips along the water until it reaches the side of the ship, drops down when it loses force, and a time-fuse explodes it below the waterline.

But how do you live long enough to get close enough to a Japanese ship to skip-bomb? Every enemy ship, including merchant vessels, had quick-firing deck guns that could tear a low-flying plane to pieces.

Kenney was puzzled and gave the problem to someone he called "a super-experimental gadgeteer and all-around fixer." Major Paul Gunn, called "Pappy" because he was over forty, had a private score to settle with the Japanese. His wife had been trapped in the Philippines by the war, and the sooner Japan was beaten the sooner "Pappy" Gunn would see her.

Gunn changed the B-25 medium bomber into a ship-destroyer. He took out the bombardier's position in the plane's nose and put in eight .50-caliber machine guns.

Then he fixed the two top turret guns to allow them to lock into a forward-firing position. At 300 feet these ten guns could hose down a ship's deck with bullets, killing its antiaircraft gunners and allowing the plane to skip bomb in safety.

Gunn's chance to test his work came soon enough. The Bismarck Sea lies to the north of New Britain and was the chief resupply route from Rabaul to New Guinea. On March 1, 1943, Kenney's planes sighted a Japanese convoy making a dash for New Guinea under the cover of bad weather.

Kenney waited, allowing the enemy ships to steam into the jaws of his trap. On March 3, he sprang it shut. A dozen B-25s escorted by P-38s raked the ships' decks with their machine guns and skip bombed. By the end of the day the Japanese had lost four destroyers, at least sixty of their covering planes, all eight of their transports, and over four thousand troops who were shot on the decks of the sinking ships or drowned. Kenney lost two bombers and three fighters.

A few days later Radio Tokyo said that Port Moresby really had no military value. Kenney and his Kids had made it possible for MacArthur to halt the Japanese advance in New Guinea and save Australia.

Yet there was plenty left to do. The airstrip the Japanese were building on Guadalcanal had to be taken before it was finished; otherwise its planes would be able to sink an invasion fleet. And so at dawn on August 7, 1942, troops of the First Marine Division stormed ashore on "The Canal," beginning one of the worst nightmares in Marine Corps history.

The first United States amphibious landing of World War II took the Japanese by surprise. The marines simply walked in and captured the unfinished airstrip, renaming it Henderson Field in honor of a United States marine flyer killed at Midway. But the enemy quickly shook off his surprise and came back like a swarm of angry bees.

The Battle of Guadalcanal began with an air fight. The marines had been ashore for only a few hours when Japanese bombers and fighters swept in from Rabaul some 650 miles to the northwest. The leathernecks had grandstand seats for the "show." Safely hidden by the jungle, they watched as the Japanese planes scrambled with the fighters from the American carriers lying offshore. Hot shell casings fell from the sky and beat on the palm leafs like raindrops. Marine old-timers clapped and whistled whenever an enemy went down trailing smoke or booed when one broke through to bomb the transports.

The Japanese tried everything to force the marines off Guadalcanal. Between August, 1942, and January, 1943, they sent the Imperial Navy down The Slot six times and each time a great sea battle broke out. So many ships sank in the waters between Guadalcanal and nearby Savo Island that the marines called the place "Ironbottom Sound." Among the navy's losses were the carriers *Hornet* and *Wasp*. The Japanese had been gunning for the "Blue Ghost" ever since the Doolittle raid and finally caught up with her.

But the marines held on. The nights on Guadalcanal were filled with terror. Marines feared the beautiful tropical sunsets, because darkness brought the "Tokyo Express," Japanese warships and reinforcements from Rabaul. The worst was the Night of the Battleships. It began normally with Louie the Louse, a Japanese scout plane, dropping his usual green flares after midnight. Then the battleships opened up ten miles away with their big guns. PAH-BOOM . . . PAH-BOOM . . . PAH-BOOM. The shells arched through the darkness like flaming boxcars. Over a thousand giant shells fell into and around Henderson Field that night.

Still the marines held on. They held on in spite of air attacks from Rabaul. They held on when fresh troops from Rabaul charged, screaming "We drink American blood!" They held on and finished the airstrip. On the evening of August 20 — thirteen days after the landing — General Alexander Vandergrift, the marine commander, was standing alongside the airstrip. He happened to look skyward. From the east, flying into the sun, he saw marine SBD dive-bombers and Wildcats. "I was close to tears and I wasn't alone," he wrote, "when the first SBD taxied up and this handsome and dashing aviator jumped to the ground. 'Thank God you have come,' I told him."

The Cactus Air Force (Guadalcanal's code name was CACTUS) was in business. The most famous squadron in the Pacific was part of this force. The squadron was called the "Black Sheep Squadron" and it was led by thirty-year-old Major Gregory "Pappy" Boyington. A short man with the arms and shoulders of a wrestler, Boyington had learned to fight the Japanese as a Flying Tiger. He learned well, shooting down twenty-eight enemy planes, more than any other Marine Corps pilot.

"Pappy" Boyington taught his Sheep to fight like Tigers: don't dog-fight the Zero, attack in pairs, hit and run. The Black Sheep became so successful that they made a strange offer. They were running out of their favorite piece of clothing: long-billed baseball caps. So they promised to shoot down a Zero for every cap they received from a major league baseball team back home. The St. Louis Cardinals sent twenty caps, in return for which the Black Sheep did even better than they had promised; they downed forty-eight enemy planes.

By February, 1943, hard-fighting leathernecks in the air and on the ground had forced the Japanese to withdraw their remaining troops from Guadalcanal. They had to bring them out at night, because the marine flyers "owned" the daytime sky.

As the tide of battle turned in the Owen Stanleys and Guadalcanal, the Joint Chiefs of Staff in Washington began to draw up plans for winning the Pacific war. Part of their plan was called Operation CARTWHEEL, and Rabaul was its target. General MacArthur's army moving along New Guinea's northern coast, and Admiral Halsey's marines coming up through the Solomons, would form the jaws of a giant nutcracker. Once they were on either side of Rabaul they would squeeze, crushing the Japanese fortress. With Rabaul out of action, United States forces would be free to cross the fifteen hundred miles of ocean that separated New Guinea from the Philippines.

MacArthur and Halsey had never met before CART-WHEEL. Yet within five minutes they felt as if they had been friends all their lives. Halsey, whose nicknames were "Bull," "Stud," and "Old Man," was just the kind of person MacArthur needed for a partner.

Each knew that fighting the Japanese in the jungle was like wrestling a crocodile in a swamp. The United

States couldn't take the losses that kind of fighting would bring and still be able to throw most of its strength against the main enemy, Germany. MacArthur and Halsey found a better, cheaper, way. Together they hammered out the method of "island hopping."

The method was always the same. Instead of attacking the enemy where he was strongest, they went for a nearby area that seemed weakly defended. A task force of about 100 to 150 ships would appear offshore one morning before dawn. Battleships and cruisers would pound the shore defenses with their big guns while destroyers fanned out to form a screen against interference from enemy ships. Carriers launched air strikes against the shore defenses and sent out patrols to take care of any Japanese planes that might want to cause trouble.

The landing troops were not supposed to capture the island right away; in fact, their real objective might be an enemy-held island several miles away. Their first task was to capture ground for an airstrip and dig in to hold what they had taken. That airstrip, and it alone, was the reason Uncle Sam had ferried them across the Pacific Ocean.

Gaining command of the air was the most important part of any Pacific battle. No island position could be captured or defended without it. The attackers needed air power to cover their fleets and troops; the defenders needed it to keep their supply lines open. Unlike land war on a continent like Europe or Africa, where some supplies always reached the defenders in spite of the Allies' control of the air, an island can be cut off completely.

Air power went ashore as soon as the landing force

secured some ground. If they captured an enemy airstrip, all well and good; planes flew in almost immediately. If there was no airstrip, only jungle, then the Seabees had their work cut out for them.

The Seabees (from CBs, Construction Battalions) were the Navy's construction workers, men who were usually too old to serve in combat units. They proudly called themselves "the toughest road gang in history." There wasn't any construction work too hard for them to tackle and to finish in record time. Give them some shovels and a bulldozer, and the "impossible" became routine for the Seabees.

Seabees' specialty. Members of the Construction Battalions use heavy equipment to build an airfield on Eniwetok Island.

Airfields were a Seabee specialty. Working around the clock, even as Japanese snipers were still taking pot-shots from the treetops, they cleared the jungle. Giant trees were cut down and the stumps blasted out with dynamite. They graded the land and filled in the swamps with anything they could find, including dead enemy soldiers. Lengths of steel mesh called "Marston mats" were then laid out on the ground, covered with crushed coral, and soaked with sea water to form a runway surface as hard as concrete. The Seabees usually finished an eight thousand-foot runway in less than three weeks.

Fighters and bombers operating from these air-fields clamped an "air blockade" around the Japanese positions, preventing them from bringing in supplies and fresh troops. Then the Americans waited for time, air strikes, and the jungle to do their work.

At first Japanese soldiers would make fun of the American planes. They could not believe that airplanes could harm them if they dug deep foxholes and cam-ouflaged themselves. A private serving in New Guinea boasted in his diary that "Japanese troops are not afraid of bombing or strafing. It is a matter of getting used to it. In the jungle one is quite safe behind tree trunks and stumps."

He was wrong. Within a few days even the simplest Japanese soldier understood what it meant to lose control of the air. An air blockade always meant starvation and disease. Finding food in the jungle is difficult. Farming is impossible, for the soil is poor. Even if it were more fertile, armies are too busy moving and fighting to plant crops. There is no big game to hunt in the jungle either. There *are* plenty of insects, but they usually take bites out of soldiers instead of the other way around. Swamp water is filled with germs, and deadly. Fresh water must be brought in by tanker or water purifying plants set up, both of which are hard to do when parafrags are falling everywhere.

The planes gave the starving soldiers no rest. Day and night, night and day, the sky was alive with American hunters. Here is what some Japanese soldiers wrote in their diaries at different times in 1943.

"I can't lift up my head because of the fierce bombing and strafing. I live in a hole and cannot speak in a loud voice. I live the life of a mud rat or some similar creature."

"I flung myself on the ground and all but cried. Every time I endure one of these bombing attacks I say to myself: 'Ah! friendly planes, fly over us:' "

On April 18, 1943, a year to the day after Doolittle's visit to Tokyo, the USAAF gave the Japanese people a painful blow. A few days earlier, MAGIC had decoded a message from Rabaul. The message said that Admiral Yamamoto would be arriving at an airfield on Bougainville in the upper Solomons on the eighteenth. He would be flying in a "Betty"* bomber and most of his staff would be in another plane. They would be escorted by six Zeros.

After much debate in the nation's capital, Frank Knox, Secretary of the Navy, radioed a message to Henderson Field, Guadalcanal. It gave details of Yama-

---

* The Americans gave men's and women's names to Japanese planes for easy identification, thus the Zero was "Zeke"; there were also Betties, Kates, Vals, and Tonies.

moto's flight plan and ordered a "maximum effort" against him. In other words, "Get Yamamoto!"

That was one of the most pleasant orders ever received at Henderson Field. Here was a chance to settle old scores and maybe shorten the war by eliminating one of Japan's chief war planners. There must be no slip-ups.

Sixteen Lightnings — a four-plane "hit" team under Captain Thomas G. Lanphier and a twelve-plane covering group — took off from Henderson Field to keep their date with the Admiral. The planes flew low, skimming the water to avoid detection. Their timing had to be perfect, for their mission was a thousand miles round trip and they couldn't wait around using up precious fuel.

Everything went like clockwork. The "hit" team tore into the Betties while their escort ran interference in a deadly shootout with the Zeros. The bombers dived to treetop level, hoping to shake off their attackers. No good. The plane with Yamamoto's staff crashed into the jungle and exploded. Captain Lanphier and his wing man, Lieutenant Rex A. Barber, dived toward Yamamoto's plane, got it in their gun sights, and fired long, steady bursts into it. The plane became a ball of flame and plunged into the jungle. Japanese searchers later found Yamamoto's body in its seat, his samurai sword still resting between his legs.

Yamamoto's death brought the war home to the Japanese people with the sharpness of a slap in the face. Until then they had been living on memories of the glorious days after Pearl Harbor. The Doolittle raid had done little damage and they could tell themselves that American bombers would never return. The defeat at Midway had been kept secret from them. But there was no way to hide Yamamoto's death. He was Japan's great man, and once his death was announced the people began to lose faith in victory.

MacArthur's and Halsey's forces were moving ever closer to Rabaul. MacArthur leapfrogged along New Guinea's north coast, putting his troops ashore, building airfields, and starving out the isolated Japanese. In December, 1943, he crossed from New Guinea to Cape Gloucester on New Britain and built air bases within easy reach of Rabaul. The Japanese sent up their planes in batches of seventy or eighty at a time and Kenney's Kids shot them down in batches.

Meanwhile, Halsey climbed the "Solomon Island ladder" up from Guadalcanal. He took the Russell Islands (February, 1943), New Georgia (June), Vella Lavella (August), Choiseul and the Treasury Islands (October), and Bougainville (December). Each victory brought his planes closer to Rabaul. Finally, in February, 1944, he took Green Island, placing his fighters only 120 miles from Rabaul's airfields and harbor.

The jaws of the nutcracker snapped shut. Planes from New Guinea, Cape Gloucester, the Solomons, Green Island, and carrier task forces blasted the Japanese stronghold without mercy. Rabaul was finished. When the last Japanese planes flew away to safety at Truk in the Caroline Islands seven hundred miles to the north, Rabaul's military importance flew away with them. About one hundred thirty-five thousand Japanese troops were left stranded in Rabaul. But without their own air support, and encircled by the United States air blockade, they were militarily harmless, and there was no reason to lose

American lives in driving them out. They marched out and surrendered by themselves when Tokyo ordered them to at the end of the war.

The Japanese planes sent to safety at Truk flew from the frying pan into the fire. For as MacArthur and Halsey closed in on Rabaul, the second part of the Joint Chiefs' plan was slipping into high gear. That plan was to advance toward Japan itself by a series of leapfrogging hops from one island chain to another. Admiral Nimitz would strike westward from Pearl Harbor with powerful sea, air, and land forces. These would slice straight across the Central Pacific, cutting through Japan's outer defense ring in the Gilbert and Marshall Islands and the inner defense ring in the Marianas and Pelau Islands. Each victory would give him bases from which to prepare the next advance. Once the Japanese home islands came into range, the Navy and Air Force would cut the enemy off from his overseas raw materials and bomb his factories.

Most of Japan's islands in the Central Pacific had been taken from Germany during the First World War, when Japan fought on the Allies' side. Japan immediately cleared them of all foreigners except for a few missionaries and spent the next twenty years preparing their defenses. Every inch of beach was covered by artillery and machine guns manned by Hirohito's best soldiers. No amount of shelling could destroy them all. The Japanese soldiers waited for the invader, comfortable in their bombproof shelters covered with thirty-five feet of steel, coral, and coconut logs.

America's "new" Pacific fleet held the key to assaulting these island fortresses. By the end of 1943 United

States shipyards were sending the most powerful fleet in the history of sea warfare to the Pacific. Soon nearly six hundred warships were cruising the "Peaceful Ocean."

The backbone of this fleet was not the big-gunned battleships, but the carriers. Nearly one hundred carriers of all sizes were in the Pacific by the time Nimitz made his move. These included a dozen giant fleet carriers and scores of escort carriers. The "baby flattops" or "jeep carriers" were small vessels that carried about fifty planes each. They could go anywhere, and go fast. Altogether the United States had more than eighteen thousand planes ready for the big push.

Nimitz moved swiftly. Makin and Tarawa in the Gilberts fell after a fierce four-day battle on November 24, 1943. The next step was the Marshalls, five hundred miles to the northwest, where the key islands of Kwajalein and Eniwetok were secured by February 21, 1944. In both the Gilberts and Marshalls nearly all the Japanese soldiers decided to die in mass *"banzai"* charges against the dug-in marines or to kill themselves rather than be captured.

These defeats were the beginning of the end of Truk seventeen hundred miles to the west. On February 17 and 18, a powerful task force under Admiral Raymond A. Spruance hit Truk, the Japanese version of Pearl Harbor. Spruance was a quiet, mild-mannered man. His class book at the U.S. Naval Academy described him as a person who would "never hurt anything or anybody except in the line of Duty." This gentle man became one of the world's masters of carrier warfare. He had been in command during the later stages of the Battle of Midway, and now was in charge of his own carrier force.

Making his approach to Truk during the height of a storm, Spruance launched his planes when the enemy least expected an attack. The few Japanese fighters that managed to get off the ground were shot down — some took off in such a hurry that ground crews hadn't time to load their machine guns. By noon the Japanese had lost 275 planes and two hundred thousand tons of shipping, compared to Spruance's loss of twenty-five planes. Truk, like Rabaul, was finished. It would be strangled by an air-sea blockade, but not invaded.

Japan's outer defense ring had collapsed and the islands of the inner ring braced for the attack that was sure to come. Their defenders didn't have to wait very long. The Marianas lie some three thousand miles west of Hawaii and thirteen hundred fifty miles south of Tokyo. They are a chain of islands of which only three — Guam, Tinian, Saipan — had any military importance. All were within bomber range of Japan, which meant that Japan would fight for them to the last.

Nimitz sent Spruance to the Marianas with 535 ships, two thousand planes, and one hundred twenty-seven thousand troops in mid-June, 1944, just as Eisenhower's forces were settling into Normandy. After a heavy air-sea bombardment, the troops landed on Saipan, June 15. Four days later a Japanese carrier force steamed into the area for a do-or-die battle.

Death it would be. Officially, what followed is known as the Battle of the Philippine Sea. But those who lived through those three days (June 19 through 21) knew it as "The Great Marianas Turkey Shoot."

There had never been such an air-sea battle; even Midway was small by comparison. This time the Americans outclassed their enemies in every way. Their pilots were better trained, coming to battle with at least two years of training and over three hundred flying hours. The Japanese pilots, however, were poor copies of those who had died at Coral Sea and Midway. With only six months of training and a few hours of flying time due to fuel shortages, they were no match for the enemy.

The Americans also had better planes. The Zero had not been improved very much since Pearl Harbor, but by 1944, the United States Navy had the best propeller-driven carrier fighter ever built. Two years earlier, the navy had captured a Zero intact when the pilot broke his neck during a landing and the plane flipped over without exploding. That Zero was shipped to the States for testing by aviation engineers, who then built a plane to have all of its advantages and none of its weaknesses.

The Grumman F6F Hellcat could outrun, outclimb, and outshoot anything the Japanese had. It was as safe as a fighter could be. The pilot sat in his cockpit protected by heavy armor plate behind the seat and by a windshield of bulletproof glass in front. "I love this plane so much," said a Navy pilot, "that if it could cook I'd marry it."

The Great Marianas Turkey Shoot was the Hellcat's first big battle. It proved itself to be as good as gold. By the end of the battle the United States had lost 130 planes — eighty of which crash-landed on carrier decks or "ditched" at sea when fuel ran out — seventy-six pilots, and three warships slightly damaged. But the Japanese fleet would never be the same. It lost two giant carriers: *Shokaku,* a veteran of Pearl Harbor, and *Taiho,* its biggest and newest carrier, plus their 346 planes and pilots. The

Turkey Shoot broke the back of Japanese naval aviation.

With their air cover gone, the defenders of Saipan knew they were lost. "It is especially pitiful that we cannot control the air," wrote Lieutenant Imanishi. "We can only clench our fists with anger and wait."

It was a short wait. Saipan fell on July 13, Tinian on August 2, and Guam on August 10. When told that it was all over in the Marianas, one of Hirohito's admirals could only say "Hell is upon us."

7

Fire from the Sky

1050 hours, October 25, 1944. Ninety miles off the eastern shore of Leyte Island, the Philippines. Visibility poor, with rain squalls and high clouds.

The crews of the five baby flattops are settling down after the All Clear. An hour earlier they had turned back the Japanese Imperial Navy's last try at breaking through the screening ships to the transports landing General MacArthur's Philippine invasion force. Men doze at their posts, too tired to drag themselves to their cots below-decks. Others hold tin mugs between greasy hands, gulping mouthfuls of steaming, ink-black coffee.

Suddenly the loudspeakers blare: "MAN YOUR BATTLE STATIONS!"

Nine Zeros are skimming the waves below radar-detection level. Sighting the carriers, they climb sharply as Hellcats streak after them. While four tangle with the stubby American fighters, the others go into sharp-angle power dives. Each has a 550-pound bomb lashed to its belly.

On they come toward the carriers. Any second now the gun crews expect to see the black blobs fall and hear the planes screech out of their dives before the explosions. Instead they gain speed, holding their course. The sweating gunners suddenly realize that these pilots don't *want* to pull out.

One dives into the port catwalk of *Kitkun Bay,* explodes, and falls into the sea. Two others blow apart before reaching *Fanshaw Bay,* victims of flak. The last two planes, one following the other, slam into the flight deck of *St. Lo,* rocking it with explosions and sending it to the bottom.

The Kamikaze Special Attack Corps has officially arrived.

That these young Japanese should have thought it necessary to kill themselves in this way tells how badly the war was going for their country as 1944 drew to a close. American commanders had moved swiftly after the Great Marianas Turkey Shoot. As Nimitz's fleet steamed southwest to capture the Palau Islands in mid-September, MacArthur and Halsey were preparing to join it for the invasion of the Philippines.

The Japanese knew that if the Philippines fell, their homeland would lose one of its most important island shields and be open to attack from almost any point of the compass. Their airmen were in a panic to find a way to turn back the enemy. Then, on October 19, Vice-Admiral Takijiro Ohnishi, commander of the Imperial Air Force in the Philippines, offered an answer at a meeting with flyers at Mabalacat Field near Manila. Ohnishi told them that the Americans could be stopped if each man crashed his bomb-carrying Zero into a carrier.

Ohnishi's idea made sense to the flyers, every one of whom volunteered for suicide duty. It made sense militarily, because there seemed no other way of halting the American drive. It also made sense in terms of *Bushido,* the code of honor of the ancient samurai warrior. *Bushido* taught that life without honor was meaningless and that "dying well" was the best thing that could happen to a samurai.

Ohnishi's men were formed into a unit known as the *Kamikaze Tokubetsu Kogekitai*. The name is very poetic and Japanese. It means Divine Wind Special Attack Corps and comes from a legend based on fact. In 1281, the emperor of China set off to conquer Japan with a huge fleet and army. The Japanese were helpless until Ise, the Sun Goddess, sent a storm to wreck the fleet. Since then the Japanese have given thanks for the *kamikaze,* or "divine wind" that saved their country.

Young Japanese thought it an honor to join the Kamikaze corps, for anyone who died for the emperor went straight to heaven and was worshipped by his ancestors. Their flight training was very simple, taking only about a week. Two days were spent on learning to take off, two on formation flying, and three on attacking a target. Landing instruction was unnecessary. His training completed, the volunteer was sent to a base to await orders. When these came he drank a cup of rice wine for

A Kamikaze pilot aims his plane at his target ship. The Kamikaze were the suicide corps used by the Japanese in the closing days of the Second World War in the hope that the heavy casualties they inflicted would discourage an American invasion of their homeland.

good luck, wrote a last letter to his parents, cried *"Banzai!"* and took off, looking for a carrier to sink.

The divine wind blew strongly off the Philippine coast. In the two months after the loss of *St. Lo,* Kamikazes sank fifteen other ships and damaged another eighty-seven, at a cost of 378 planes and flyers. Yet no major warship was sunk or put out of action for long. These young men gave their lives, and took many young American lives, but they couldn't slow down MacArthur.

Even before the end of the battle for the Philippines in January, 1945, another threat to the home islands began. The Americans called this threat B-29, or Superfortress.

The B-29 was Hap Arnold's brainchild. The idea went back to the end of 1939, when FDR was demanding planes and lots of them. Arnold told his engineers at Wright Field, Dayton, Ohio, to design a superbomber and "make them the biggest, gun them the heaviest, and fly them the farthest" of any plane in history.

Working in total secrecy, 750 engineers drew up blueprints in two years, a record time; the USAAF accepted its first Superfortress on July 29, 1943. The plane went into mass production in five factories where the employees worked in shifts around the clock. By the end of 1944, they were turning out six planes every day, or 1664 by the time the Japanese surrendered. The cost per plane fell from exactly $3,392,396.60 for the test model to under $600,000 for the last in the series.

Hap Arnold's gamble paid off just when Uncle Sam needed it most. The B-29 was not simply "another bomber." It stood in a class by itself. Although propeller-driven, its design and equipment made it a closer relative of the supersonic jet bombers of the future than the Flying Fortresses and Liberators of its own day.

BIG! That was the only word for it. The Super-fortress's fuselage was a gracefully rounded ninety-nine-foot cylinder; its wings measured 141 feet from tip to tip. Four twenty-two-hundred horsepower Wright Cyclone engines, each whirling a four-bladed propeller, could lift its sixty tons of fighting machinery to thirty-eight thousand feet.

Superfortress crewmen payed no attention to cold at high altitudes. Wearing only their uniforms, they sat comfortably in the plane's pressurized compartments warmed by the hot air from the motors. Those mighty motors allowed the B-29, the world's first intercontinental bomber, to fly on thirty-two-hundred fifty-mile missions lasting sixteen hours. And the plane was fast — faster even than some of the best fighters. The Superfortress could fly at 365 miles an hour at twenty-five thousand feet, while the improved Zero could do only 351 miles an hour at nineteen thousand seven hundred feet. Its *normal* bombload was ten tons, meaning that each plane could shower a target with forty 500-pounders or two hundred 100-pound fire bombs.

The Superfortress was an electronic marvel. The first plane with CFC (Central Fire Control), it had a defense system operated by computer. The only decision a gunner had to make was which weapons to use; the computer did the rest. It locked onto the enemy fighter, measuring its speed, distance, and angle of approach. Using this information, it calculated the effects of wind, temperature, and gravity on the bullets, then ordered the guns to cut loose.

The Superfortress had five gun turrets: two on top,

The B-29 Superfortress was the largest propeller-driven plane ever used in warfare. Its range, bomb load, and fire control system made it the ideal strategic bomber in the campaign against Japan's home islands.

two underneath, one in the tail. The upper forward turret had four big fifties, the others two each. The tail carried a scorpion's sting: a cannon flanked by machine guns.

The gunners sat in five sighting positions away from

their weapons. No more crouching for hours behind the tail guns, or scrunching into the ball turret. There was no ball turret. A turret-switching system allowed one gunner to control several turrets if the plane was attacked from his side or if another gunner was out of action. Taking over another turret was as easy as flicking a switch.

By the spring of 1944, the USAAF was getting ready to use its new weapon. In April it began to build five airfields near Calcutta, India. These were to be the B-29s' rear base area, where planes and crews were readied before being sent to forward bases at Chengtu in western China. From there they would be able to bomb the Japanese home islands.

General Curtis E. LeMay, who had led one of the Eighth's air divisions over Germany, was put in charge at Chengtu. His jaw must have sagged when he saw the place for the first time. For Chengtu had no airfields nor the machines for building them. But there were people, lots of hardworking Chinese who wanted to see those great planes winging toward Japan. Over a half-million Chinese went to work under the direction of American engineers. Young men and girls, bearded grandfathers,

Chinese workers pulling a stone roller over a B-29 runway. Without heavy construction machinery such as the Seabees had, muscle power alone had to construct facilities for the giant bombers.

mothers with babies strapped to their backs, children: everyone pitched in to build airstrips.

They worked with simple tools or with only their bare hands. They broke millions of pounds of rock with hammers, carried the material in buckets or baskets on their backs, and laid the stones by hand. Thousands of men then tied themselves to stone rollers and pulled them to flatten the runways.

Supplies were harder to find than laborers. The B-29 was a complicated aircraft. It had over fifty-five thousand numbered parts, each of which wore out and needed replacing from time to time. Those spare parts, plus fuel, bombs, and everything else had to come through a ten-thousand-mile supply line stretching from California across the Pacific to Calcutta. There the supplies were unloaded from ships and loaded onto B-29s for the flight over the "Hump," the highest part of the Himalaya Mountains between India and China. It took seven B-29 flights

General Curtis E. LeMay, commander of B-29
Superfortresses in China and, later, in the Marianas,
with General Roger M. Ramey.

to bring in enough supplies for one B-29's combat mission
to Japan.

On June 5, 1944, a day before the Allies stormed
ashore in Normandy, LeMay's planes went into action
with attacks on railroad targets in Thailand. Ten days

later the Japanese had the shock of their lives. For the first time since Doolittle they saw USAAF bombers flying through their skies. No one waved this time. Those on the ground heard the planes before they saw them. First came the thundering of engines, then the V's soaring overhead. Sixty-eight of the silvery planes released long strings of high explosive on the Imperial Steel Works on the island of Kyushu.

Other raids followed; yet it was hard to keep up the pace because the big bombers quickly outran their supplies. They would have to be moved closer to Japan and to their supply lines.

As soon as the Marianas had been captured plans were made to bring in new B-29s from the United States and to transfer the others from India and China. Again, the problem was airfields. The former Japanese fields were of no use for Superfortresses. A Superfortress needed a runway eighty-five hundred feet long by 200 feet wide, and these were nowhere nearly as large. The only thing to do was to build in the Marianas five of the largest airports in the world, and do so in under three months.

The USAAF's Engineer Aviation Battalions, the Navy's Seabees, and the Army's Engineers moved in their heavy machinery and got down to business. In order to move the millions of cubic yards of coral needed to surface Isley Field, Saipan, engineers attacked two coral *mountains* with bulldozers and steamshovels. The mountains disappeared, ground up by the steel jaws of the earth movers. The Negro engineers of the 1849th Battalion built a three-lane highway in three days so that the trucks could haul the coral from the quarry to the building site.

Meanwhile work on each of Guam's and Tinian's two airfields was moving along. Each job had its own special problems. On Tinian, for instance, one runway had to cross a valley; the valley was filled in, leveled, and surfaced with tar over steel mesh.

Tinian was a sight to cheer a New Yorker. Its roads and streets were laid out along the lines of Manhattan Island, with numbered avenues running north and south and numbered east-west "crosstown" streets. The tent city of the 509th Composite Bomb Group was near "Times Square." Soon the whole world would learn the secret of the 509th's mission.

By the end of October, 1944, the Marianas' fields were almost complete. Brigadier General Hayward S. "Possom" Hansell flew the first B-29, *Joltin' Josie, the Pacific Pioneer,* into Saipan. After some training raids on Iwo Jima and Truk, on November 24, he led the first Marianas-based Superfortresses — 110 of them — on the skyroad to Tokyo. Practically every day from then on more B-29s came winging in over the Pacific to their new bases until 985 planes were on hand.

Hansell began to bomb Japan's factory towns about once every five days. Yet results were disappointing. Japanese war production was being hurt, but nowhere near what the B-29's supporters had promised. One reason was that the enemy always knew when an attack was coming. Although the Marianas had been captured, there were still plenty of Japanese soldiers around. Rather than surrender or commit suicide, at least a thousand of them hid in caves, especially on Saipan. A few had radios and would call Tokyo whenever a lot of bombers took off. If they failed to get in touch, there was always Iwo Jima some 575 miles to the north. The Japanese base there had a powerful radar station that told Tokyo about the B-29 formations' course and altitude.

Loss of surprise, though, was not the only problem. American airmen ran into jet streams, fierce winds that blow above twenty-five thousand feet, for the first time during the B-29 raids. Miles above Japan, winds blow harder than any place on earth. Winds of more than two hundred miles an hour are common. As the bombers neared the Japanese coast, strong headwinds held them motionless in the air, or forced them back tail first over the Pacific. And the stronger the winds, the more gasoline the planes used, lessening their time over the target and making the return flight risky.

The Japanese pilot fighting over his homeland was another problem. The German pilot was daring, even reckless, but he tried to come out of battle in one piece. The Japanese pilot didn't care what happened to him as long as he brought down a Superfortress. He pressed his attacks right down a formation's line of fire. Or he flew straight at a bomber, locked his controls, and bailed out a split second before the crash. Often he didn't bother to bail out, but died Kamikaze-style.

Superfortresses returning from the Empire, as the airmen called Japan, had their hands full. Gas was low. Planes trailed the formation or "ditched" because of battle damage. As they neared Iwo Jima, fighters rose from its three fields to pick off the stragglers.

Iwo Jima was a thorn in the side of the USAAF that had to be removed. Lying only 775 miles from Japan,

Iwo Jima is a bare volcanic island only eight square miles in area — and the Japanese fought for every square inch of those eight square miles. After twenty-six days of desperate fighting, the marines secured the island on March 16, 1945. "The fighting was the toughest the marines ran across in 168 years," said Lieutenant General Holland M. "Howling Mad" Smith, who commanded the landing force.

The price of Iwo Jima was high — 6,821 dead Americans — but so were the benefits. The Japanese no longer had advance warning of B-29 raids and swarms of Mustangs escorted their "big friends" from the island's airstrips. Best of all, Iwo Jima was an emergency landing place halfway on the long road back from the Empire to the Marianas. During the six months between its capture and the war's end, 24,761 Superfortress crewmen used its airfields when their planes developed trouble.

But the main reason for the B-29s' failure to destroy Japan's war industries was the targets themselves. High-altitude precision daylight bombing worked against Germany because its factories were large buildings of steel and concrete. High explosive bombs with steel tips to break through the roofs were effective against such targets. They were wasted against Japan, which had few large factories that could build a weapon from start to finish. Japan depended instead on many small "feeder" industries. Her factories were surrounded by wood and plaster slum buildings, the homes of the workers themselves. Their neighborhoods never slept. Day and night they hummed with the activity of thousands of "shadow factories." A shadow factory was a small shop set up in a worker's home. Each shop had a lathe, or a punch, or some other machine for working metal.

In Japan the worker's whole family was a cog in the war machine. They were soldiers of the home front who sweated long hours in their home shops to produce weapons parts. These parts were then carried in a sack on someone's back to the neighborhood factory to be put together as a complete weapon.

How could you tell from thirty thousand feet which home was a shadow factory? And even if you could tell, a steel-tipped bomb would only break through the roof and bury itself in the earth, smothering the blast.

General LeMay replaced Hansell on January 20, 1945. The word went out: "Iron Pants" LeMay was coming to the Marianas. What LeMay had in mind for Japan was really "hot stuff."

The odor of sweat hung heavily in the tropical air as the crews crowded into the briefing rooms on the morning of March 9, 1945. Everything seemed normal: the rows of wooden benches, the maps on the walls, the little stage for the officers. It was hot and everyone dressed informally in khaki shorts and open shirts.

Almost at the exact moment on Saipan, Tinian, and Guam, the group commanders strolled in with their staffs. The men stood up and snapped to attention. Then everyone sat, except the group commanders.

They stepped to the edge of the stage. Each used different words, but what they said was the same: Everything would be different in the next B-29 raid, scheduled for Tokyo that evening.

Evening! That's a new one. Heavy bomber raids were always in daylight to allow the bombardiers to pinpoint the target. Everyone began to listen more carefully.

The Superfortresses would go to the target singly. No assembly. No formations. No combat boxes. Just each plane on its own.

The men leaned forward puzzled — and scared. The high-flying bombers would not fly high this time. They would come down from thirty-five thousand feet to attack from between five and seven thousand feet. A B-29 is a big airplane and at that low altitude would be a wonderfully large target for flak gunners.

The Germans defended their cities with two kinds of flak: heavy .88s and light twenty- and thirty-seven-millimeter cannon. When a plane flew in low over Germany it was safe from the big stuff, because the gunners couldn't adjust their sights fast enough. But the lighter guns would tear a formation apart. Luckily, LeMay didn't think the Japanese had many light flak guns, so there shouldn't be any problem.

That first night they were to drop incendiaries. The Superfortresses would be stripped of all unnecessary weight to make room for more fire bombs.

"Unnecessary" weight meant machine guns and ammunition. A B-29 carried about thirty-two hundred pounds of ammunition, weight that could better be given to bombs. All weapons except the tail cannon would be left behind this time; on future missions it would be left behind also. Darkness and speed would be the raiders' only protection.

Shocked silence turned into curses as the crews

LeMay's big gamble. Superfortresses on the runway, waiting to take off for the great Tokyo fire raid of March 9, 1945.

began to realize what LeMay had in mind. Without guns it would be suicide! No, it would be *murder!*

The men grumbled as they climbed into their planes hours later. Before dusk 334 Superfortresses took off, one every thirty seconds, from Saipan, Tinian, and Guam. Packed into their bomb bays was a load equal to that of one thousand Flying Fortresses. It would be a long night.

The bombers thundered across the Pacific. Northward, always northward, they streamed, passing Iwo Jima. The sun set to their left, plunging them into a blackness broken only by the canopy of stars above.

Up ahead two lone B-29s had already crossed the Japanese coast. The sky was clear with only scattered clouds. These were the Pathfinders, and they needed good visibility, for they would find the heart of Tokyo and "mark" it for the main force coming in behind them.

1215, March 10, 1945. The Pathfinders had no trouble finding what they were looking for. Racing toward their target at over three hundred miles an hour, the first plane dropped a string of 100-pound napalm bombs. Napalm is jellied gasoline; it burns at a temperature of over one thousand degrees and sticks like glue to anything it touches.

Moments later the second plane raced in, crossing the first's trail as it released another string of napalm bombs. When the Pathfinders flew off, they left behind a rough burning X in Tokyo's heart.

X marked the spot. A steady wind was blowing in Tokyo as the bomber stream sighted its aiming point. For the next three hours the Superfortresses would dump their fire bombs on the target. It was impossible to miss.

Back on Guam General LeMay was worried. Hours had passed since the last plane had taken off. They should have begun bombing by now and reported back to him, he thought.

Nothing. Each time LeMay walked into the radio room the operator shook his head and said nothing had come in yet.

The general had risked $400 million worth of airplanes and over three thousand American lives. He sat down in the darkness alone, chewing the end of a cigar and taking sips of Coca Cola.

Far away Tokyo was burning. Within a half hour after the first fire bombs fell, the blaze was out of control. Crews in the early planes saw thousands of tiny lights flickering below like candles. These quickly joined to become the greatest fire ever made by human beings.

Imagine a tidal wave at sea whipped onward by a strong wind. It sweeps ahead at terrific speed, washing away everything in its path.

Now imagine that wave as a fire boiling along at fifty miles an hour and whipped onward by tornado winds. That was Tokyo: a city caught in front of a tidal wave of fire burning at eighteen hundred degrees Fahrenheit.

The fiery wave slashed forward, giving off so much heat that things in its path burst into flame even before the flames reached them. Nothing could stop it. The paint on fire engines blistered in the heat and flared. The metal began to melt, while the gasoline in their tanks exploded, sending tongues of flame over the rooftops. Fire hoses shriveled like earthworms trapped in the sun after a rain. Water in some small canals boiled before turning to steam.

And still the radio at LeMay's headquarters was silent. Could he have lost his gamble? Could *all* his planes have gone down?

Then at 0121 the radio began to crackle. Everything was okay, the message said: little flak, few fighters, an unbelievable fire. The later bombers had no trouble finding Tokyo; they could see the fire from 150 miles away.

The city of Toyama was nearly ninety-five percent
destroyed during a one-night raid by LeMay's bombers,
August 1, 1945.

LeMay had won. He had lost nine Superfortresses, but over eighty-four thousand Japanese had died and a million were made homeless in a single night. About sixteen square miles were burned out of the heart of Tokyo. Those who visited the place after the war saw drill presses and other machines sticking up through the ashes of each home. During the days and weeks that followed, LeMay put the factory cities of Japan to the torch one by one.

Japan's war industries might have been grinding to a halt, but her fighting spirit was as strong as ever. "This is a sacred war against the diabolical Americans" became a national slogan. So did "Better to die than to seek dishonorable safety."

The Japanese showed how serious they were three weeks after the Tokyo raid. Even as LeMay was planning more fire storms, United States forces leapfrogged west from Iwo Jima to Okinawa, the largest island in the Ryukyu chain. Okinawa, a big island with a good harbor and airfields, was only 350 miles southwest of Japan.

The United States had to have Okinawa as a springboard for invading Japan. Here it could gather its troops and build its supply dumps. From here its fighters and bombers could cover the assault forces on Japan's invasion beaches.

The Japanese high command knew Okinawa's value and meant to keep it out of American hands. They planned to show the enemy some new tricks. The landing would not be opposed. They'd let the marines and army land, draw them inland, and then attack. Meanwhile,

Japanese ships and planes would cut off the invaders by destroying their fleet offshore.

The first part of Nimitz's one hundred eighty thousand-man invasion force went ashore on the morning of April Fools' Day, 1945, thus beginning an eighty-two-day battle. For a while the United States commanders seemed the fools for gathering so large an invasion force. The troops went in "standing up," not like at Tarawa or Iwo Jima. Everything was so easy, and by the end of the first day they had captured the island's main airstrip without firing a shot. Five days went by, and still no sign of the Japanese army. Okinawa, they said, was "the screwiest place in the Pacific."

They changed their minds the next day, April 6. On that day the Japanese made the marines pay, and pay heavily, for the easy time they had had. From then on they had to fight for every hole in the ground.

The Japanese army's attack was followed up by a one-two punch from the navy. On April 7, the last sea-air battle of World War II was fought when the Imperial Navy sent the battleship *Yamato* and nine smaller vessels to smash the American fleet. *Yamato* had been Admiral Yamamato's flagship. At 64,170 tons, it was the largest warship ever built. Its 18.1-inch guns would throw a shell weighing a ton twenty-three miles, far outdistancing anything the United States Navy had.

Soon the Japanese Navy would have nothing like *Yamato* either. She and her sister ships were gigantic floating Kamikazes. They had been loaded with ammunition and sent to sea with only enough fuel oil to reach Okinawa. There they would fight, disable the Americans, and die honorably.

Admiral Marc A. Mitscher, commander of the carrier force and its fifteen hundred planes, didn't allow the Japanese to do either. His planes found *Yamato* and circled it as sharks circle a wounded whale. Then nearly three hundred dive-bombers and torpedo planes rushed in at the same time. After four hours of pounding *Yamato* slid under; five other ships also went down that day. The navy that had pulled off the military miracle of Pearl Harbor was finished near its own coast.

Yet the divine wind blew hot and often at Okinawa in the weeks that followed. The Kamikaze tried something new. *Kikusui* is a pretty word, meaning "floating chrysanthimum," a sacred flower to the Japanese. At Okinawa, though, *kikusui* tactics were a series of mass suicide attacks by waves of planes. Their targets were, first, the small radar picket ships that surrounded the American fleet. These were the fleet's eyes; destroy them and the big carriers would be blind. Attacks on the picket ships grew so heavy that one seaman put up a sign with an arrow and the words "THAT WAY TO THE CARRIERS."

The Kamikaze found the carriers easily enough, especially those with Admiral Mitscher aboard. His flagship, the brand-new fleet carried *Bunker Hill,* was cruising under low clouds on May 11, when a Kamikaze crashed into the planes crowding its flight deck. The ship burned for many hours until Damage Control could gain the upper hand. Even so, *Bunker Hill* suffered 373 dead, 119 missing, and 264 wounded.

Mitscher was angry as he transferred his flag to the *Enterprise*, the veteran of the Pacific Fleet. *Enterprise* had destroyed seventy enemy warships and shot down over one thousand planes during her years of service. Six times the Japanese reported her sunk, and six times she fooled them. Then, on May 14, they almost had their wish. A Zero pilot dove his plane into her, penetrating three decks. The explosion sent Number 1 elevator — thirty tons of steel — hundreds of feet into the air. The "Lucky E" spent the rest of the war in a dockyard under repair.

The Kamikaze had taken a heavy toll. In all, over three thousand suicide planes hit the Americans off Okinawa, sinking twenty-one ships, turning forty-three others into scrap, and putting twenty-three out of action for a month or more. Yet they had not sunk a single major warship. No fleet carrier, no battleship, no cruiser went under because of them. The Battle of Okinawa ended, leaving twelve thousand five hundred dead American soldiers and sailors; one hundred seven thousand Japanese died on this island alone.

Nothing could stop the Americans now. Their naval and air power, spearheaded by the B-29s, was strangling the Empire. The Superfortresses dropped mines into every Japanese harbor, completing the largest blockade in history. The fire raids also continued, doing ever more damage as the airmen became more skilled.

Yet the Joint Chiefs of Staff in Washington were afraid. They knew that Japan could be invaded and would be defeated. But what would an invasion cost? The Marianas, Iwo Jima, and Okinawa had taught them a terrible lesson. Instead of the Japanese giving up when their inner defense ring was broken, they fought harder. Each battle was worse than the one before it. And now the plan was to land on Japan's own "sacred" soil in the fall of 1945.

Military men knew what the Japanese had in store for them when they came ashore. The whole Japanese nation was being prepared for Kamikaze duty. Everyone who could carry a weapon was drafted into the Home Guard; the millions who couldn't be given guns were given bamboo spears and told to make mass attacks on the American machine guns and tanks. Worst of all, the Japanese navy had thousands of "sea-shakers," manned torpedoes and motorboats loaded with dynamite, which their crews would crash into American ships. As many as ten thousand Kamikaze planes were hidden in caves or camouflaged. The plan was to use these in waves of four hundred an hour against the invasion fleet and the beachheads.

United States experts expected losses that would make D-Day in Europe seem like a picnic. General Mac-Arthur thought fifty thousand Americans would be killed or wounded on the first day of the invasion of Japan. By the time the enemy was defeated, probably late in 1946, over a million Americans would be casualties. As many as ten million Japanese were expected to die or be hurt in the battle.

This never happened because of work that had been going on for five years in scientific laboratories. Scientists from all over the world had come to the United States to work on a top-secret device they called "the gadget." The idea for the gadget had been suggested to FDR by Dr. Albert Einstein, the greatest scientist of the twentieth century. Einstein believed that a new type of explosive could be made from a rare metal called uranium. This explosive would be so powerful that its force would have to be measured not in pounds of TNT but in *thousands of tons* of it. The time was August, 1939, and FDR knew what someone like Hitler would do if his scientists developed this explosive first. Everything had to be done to make sure that the Allies had the atomic bomb before anyone else.

A secret organization was set up to do the work under the code name "Manhattan Project." Before it finished, it would have one hundred sixty-five thousand workers, only twelve of whom knew what the project was about. Everything was so secret that even the vice-president of the United States wasn't told about it. Only after FDR died in April, 1945, did Harry S Truman learn what the scientists were doing.

Over two billion dollars was spent to build huge factories in the United States. Separated from each other by thousands of miles, these factories produced enough pure uranium and another substance called plutonium for three bombs. Meanwhile, Dr. J. Robert Oppenheimer and his staff were designing the bomb itself in a secret city built in the middle of the New Mexico desert. Los Alamos had to be far away from other cities for secrecy and because the whole place might accidentally blow up.

On July 16, 1945, the first countdown of the atomic age began in an out-of-the-way corner of Alamagordo Air Base, New Mexico. At 0530, as the sun began to look over the horizon, the gadget went off. A ball of fire and smoke rose more than eight miles over the desert. The flash was seen in Amarillo, Texas, 450 miles to the east. People at El Paso, Texas, 150 miles to the south saw the flash and heard the blast; the army told them an ammunition train had exploded. Windows rattled at Gallup, New Mexico, 235 miles to the northwest. The 100-foot steel tower that had held the test bomb disappeared without a trace. The sand around where the tower had stood was turned into green glass by the heat of the explosion and could be seen from five miles away.

News of the test reached President Truman at Potsdam, Germany, where the last Allied conference of the war was being held. The message was short and said: "BABIES SATISFACTORILY BORN." "Baby" had given off the power of twenty thousand tons of TNT.

Now what? Should this awful weapon be used?

The Allied leaders were sure that it should be used if the Japanese refused to surrender. Not using it to end the war would cost millions of more lives in an invasion. On July 27, they broadcast a warning: Japan must surrender or face "complete destruction." Japan did not reply, so Truman ordered the atomic bomb to be dropped as soon as possible.

The USAAF had been preparing to deliver the weapon for a long time. The 509th Composite Bomb Group had been in training since the winter of 1944. Its eighteen hundred pilots, crewmen, and mechanics were the best anywhere. They had been taken from units all over the world and brought together into the 509th, that's why it was a "composite" group.

No one in the 509th knew what they had been chosen to do except its commander, Colonel Paul W. Tibbetts, Jr., who had been personally chosen for the mission by General Arnold. He had piloted the first B-17 to cross the English Channel to bomb German-occupied France. He had led other missions over Germany and led the first B-17s over North Africa. He was one of the most experienced airmen in the USAAF.

Tibbetts trained the 509th at an airbase in the Utah desert, far from prying eyes. When it was ready, the whole group flew to North Field, Tinian, in May, 1945. Still no one but Tibbetts knew the mission. All his men knew was that the 509th was cut off from the rest of the base by high barbed wire fences, and the the whole area around "Times Square" was patrolled by armed guards.

The 509th were prisoners, but busy ones. Every morning a three-plane formation took off, flew to Japan, dropped a single bomb, dove steeply to pick up speed, made a sharp right turn, and raced back to Tinian. The crews didn't know it, but they were getting the Japanese used to seeing small B-29 formations that did little damage; maybe they wouldn't open fire when the plane carrying the gadget flew over. The crews were also practicing a quick getaway, because the plane that dropped the atomic bomb would be in danger from its explosion.

The other bomb groups told jokes about the 509th. While they bombed the Empire, the 509th seemed to be playing games. As one poem said:

> *Into the air the secret rose,*
> *Where they are going, nobody knows.*
> *Tomorrow they'll return again,*
> *But we'll never know where they've been.*
> *Don't ask us about results as such,*
> *Unless you want to get in Dutch.*
> *But take it from one who is sure of the score,*
> *The 509th is winning the war.*

To make them even more uncomfortable, Radio Tokyo began wondering why the 509th was letting others do their fighting.

Colonel Tibbets and his men posed for pictures and then, as Tooey Spaatz and other officers looked on, climbed into their plane. It was named *Enola Gay* after Tibbets's mother, but on the nose was a lipstick kiss covered with shellac and signed "Dottie." She had been someone's girl-friend back in Utah.

At exactly 0245 on the morning of August 6, 1945, *Enola Gay* and her two escorts began to taxi; these planes were filled with photographic and scientific equipment to measure the blast. Everyone was nervous. The night before four B-29s had failed to take off, crashing and exploding in the sea or on the beach.

Faster and faster *Enola Gay* sped down the runway, but she didn't rise. Onlookers began to squirm as they saw Tibbets quickly running out of runway. He knew he had better lift her and soon; there was a nasty package nestled in his ship's bomb bay. It was black and made of steel and looked queer for a bomb. The scientists who had put it together called it "Little Boy." It was ten feet long, twenty-eight inches wide, and weighed almost nine thousand pounds!

With only a few feet to spare, *Enola Gay* left the ground with a roar and vanished into the darkness. North-ward she flew, her destination Hiroshima on Honshu, Japan's main island. Hiroshima means "the broad island." Old Hiroshima was built on a triangle of land where the seven branches of the Ota River flow into the sea. It was Japan's seventh largest city, with a population of three

"Little Boy," the atomic bomb used against Hiroshima, August 6, 1945. The bomb was ten feet long and twenty-eight inches wide; it weighed about 9,000 pounds.

"Fat Man," the atomic bomb dropped on Nagasaki, August 8, 1945. This weapon was more complicated than "Little Boy," requiring specially widened bomb bays to allow it to be dropped from a Superfortress.

hundred thousand. It had never been bombed before, and the workers in its oil refineries, warehouses, and naval installations thought their city had a charmed life. Some said the Americans would never bomb Hiroshima because General MacArthur's mother was Japanese and she lived nearby.

At 0915 people on their way to work in Hiroshima looked up to see a lone Superfortress overhead. Why worry, if it is just one plane?

At that moment "Little Boy" fell out of *Enola Gay*'s bomb bay. It fell to fifteen hundred feet above the city and then air pressure gauges set off a small charge of chemical explosive inside the bomb. The explosion shot a small plug of uranium down a gun barrel into a larger piece of uranium at the other end. When the two pieces met there was a flash, and an explosion equal to at least twenty thousand tons of TNT hit Hiroshima.

Captain Robert A. Lewis, Tibbets's co-pilot, scribbled two words in the diary he was keeping. They were "My God!"

Down below no one was writing. A Japanese reporter later told what happened:

"Suddenly a glaring whitish pinkish light appeared in the sky accompanied by an unnatural tremor, which was followed almost immediately by a wave of suffocating heat and a wind which swept away everything in its path.

"Within a few seconds thousands of people in the streets and the gardens in the center of the town were scorched by a wave of searing heat. . . . Everything standing upright in the way of the blast — walls, houses, factories, and other buildings — was annihilated and the debris spun around in a whirlwind and carried up into the air. Trams were picked up and tossed aside as though they had neither weight nor solidity. Trains were flung off the rails as though they were toys. Horses, dogs and cattle suffered the same fate as human beings. Every living thing was petrified in an attitude of indescribable suffering. Even the vegetation did not escape. Trees went up in flames, the rice plants lost their greenness, the grass burned on the ground like dry straw. . . .

"About half an hour after the explosion, while the sky all around Hiroshima was still cloudless, a fine rain began to fall on the town and went on for about five minutes. It was caused by the sudden rise of overheated air to a great height, where it condensed and fell back as rain. Then a violent wind rose and the fires extended with terrible rapidity, because most Japanese houses are built only of timber and straw.

"By the evening the fire began to die down and then it went out. There was nothing left to burn. Hiroshima had ceased to exist."

At least seventy-eight thousand people died in Hiroshima that day; another ten thousand were never found, and thirty-seven thousand more were injured.

And still Japan's warlords would not surrender. They would fight on even if that meant the end of the Japanese people. Some officers were even prepared to overthrow Emperor Hirohito if he stood in their way.

On August 9, another atomic bomb was dropped. This bomb weighed ten thousand pounds and was named "Fat Man." The target city was Nagasaki, an important

The mushroom cloud over Nagasaki.

Nagasaki in ruins after "Fat Man" did its work.

factory city and naval base. Another forty thousand people died and twenty-five thousand were injured.

And still the warlords would not surrender. Some army and navy leaders begged the Emperor to let them have "one last battle" to punish the enemy. But Hirohito wanted to save the nation's life. On August 25, the Son of Heaven spoke to his people over the radio for the first time. People bowed to their radio sets as his high-pitched voice came over the airwaves. He told them they must "bear the unbearable"—surrender.

No one had to explain the meaning of the atomic bomb to the American troops aboard the crowded transports heading for Okinawa. It meant one less predawn bombardment and one less race to a beach. It meant a chance to live. The atomic bomb brought peace to a world that had known too much war. It brought peace then, but it also announced a new terror for the world.

The last scene of World War II took place aboard the battleship *Missouri* anchored in Tokyo Bay on September 2. As representatives of the Allied powers looked on, Japanese government leaders signed the official surrender papers.

"These proceedings are closed," General MacArthur said in a steely voice. As the Japanese were being led away, he walked over to Admiral Halsey. Putting his arm around Halsey's shoulder, he said "Bill, where are those airplanes?" At that instant, as if on cue, thousands of planes — B-29s and navy carrier planes — flew across the sky.

And so the most terrible war in history ended as it had begun: with the roar of airplane motors.

Some More Books

ARNOLD, HENRY H. *Global Mission.* New York: Harper & Bros., 1949.

BELOTE, J. H. *Titans of the Seas.* New York: Harper and Row, 1975.

CAIDIN, MARTIN. *Black Thursday.* New York: E. P. Dutton & Co., Inc., 1960.

————. *A Torch to the Enemy.* New York: Ballantine Books, Inc., 1960.

CRAVEN, W. F., AND CATE, J. L., editors. *The Army Air Forces in World War II* (7 volumes). Chicago: University of Chicago Press, 1948–1958.

FRANKLAND, NOBLE. *The Bombing Offensive Against Germany.* London: Faber and Faber, 1965.

FREEMAN, R. A. *The Mighty Eighth.* Garden City, NY: Doubleday & Co., Inc., 1970.

GALLAND, ADOLF. *The First and the Last.* New York: Bantam Books, Inc., 1979.

GREEN, W. *Famous Bombers of World War II.* Garden City, NY: Doubleday & Co., Inc., 1965.

———. *Famous Fighters of World War II.* Garden City, NY: Doubleday & Co., Inc., 1957.

GURNEY, GENE. *The War in the Air.* New York: Crown Publishers, Inc., 1962.

INOGUCHI, R. *The Divine Wind: Japan's Kamikaze Force in World War II.* New York: Bantam Books, Inc., 1978.

JABLONSKI, EDWARD. *Airwar.* Garden City, NY: Doubleday & Co., Inc., 1971.

———. *Flying Fortress.* Garden City, NY: Doubleday & Co., Inc., 1965.

LEMAY, CURTIS E. *Mission with LeMay.* Garden City, NY: Doubleday & Co., Inc., 1965.

MUNSON, K. G. *Aircraft of World War II.* Garden City, NY: Doubleday & Co., Inc., 1972.

PEASLEE, B. J. *Heritage of Valor.* Philadelphia: J. B. Lippincott Co., 1964.

SIMS, E. H. *American Aces in Great Fighter Battles of World War II.* New York: Bantam Books, Inc., 1978.

———. *The Fighter Pilots.* New York: Harper & Row, 1967.

———. *The Greatest Aces.* New York: Harper & Row, 1967.

STEINBECK, JOHN. *Bombs Away: The Story of a Bomber Team.* New York: The Viking Press, 1942.

SUNDERMAN, J. F. *World War II in the Air: Europe.* New York: Bramhall House, 1963.

————. *World War II in the Air: The Pacific*. New York: Bramhall House, 1962.

TOLAND, JOHN. *The Flying Tigers*. New York: Random House, Inc., 1963.

WAGNER, RAY. *American Combat Planes*. Garden City, NY: Doubleday & Co., Inc., 1968.

WEBSTER, SIR CHARLES AND FRANKLAND, NOBLE. *The Strategic Bombing Offensive Against Germany* (4 volumes). London: Her Majesty's Stationery Office, 1961.

Index

Abbeville Kids, 44
airplanes:
  mass production methods,
    13–15
  British types: Halifax, 26,
    106; Hurricane, 25;
    Lancaster, 26, 41, 106;
    Spitfire, 25, 58, 59;
    Sterling, 26, 106;
    Typhoon, 112
  German types: Focke-
    Wulf FW-190, 23, 62,
    65, 68, 73, 76, 78, 82,
    95, 99, 109; Junkers
    Ju-87 ("Stuka"), 22;
    Junkers JU-88, 23, 67,
    88; Messerschmitt
    ME-109, 23, 25, 62,
    65, 70, 80, 95; ME-110,
    63; ME-262, 100, 101;
    ME-410, 68
  Japanese types: Zero,
    124–125, 140, 155, 156,
    166, 168, 173

United States types, A-20
  Boston; B-17 Flying
  Fortress, 18, 30, 32, 37,
  38, 40, 48, 53, 54, 59,
  61, 66, 68, 69, 70, 80,
  88, 92, 102, 110, 149;
  B-24 Liberator, 30, 47,
  84, 88, 110; B-25
  Mitchell, 128, 152, 153;
  B-29 Superfortress, 33,
  172–175, 180–184, 192;
  F6F Hellcat, 166, 169;
  P-38 Lightning, 95, 98,
  101, 149, 153; P-40
  Tomahawk, 123, 124,
  125; P-47 Thunderbolt,
  94, 101, 109, 112; P-51
  Mustang, 95, 101, 102,
  113, 182
American Volunteer Group,
  see Flying Tigers
ARCADIA Conference, 19,
  20, 34
Arnold, General Henry H.